RHYTHM: ONE on ONE

DALCROZE ACTIVITIES in the PRIVATE MUSIC LESSON

Julia Schnebly-Black, Ph.D.
and Stephen F. Moore, Ph.D.

Copyright © MMIV by
Alfred Publishing Co., Inc.
All rights reserved.
Printed in USA.

DEDICATION

To our students.

Their musical needs, errors, and accomplishments are the source and inspiration of this book.

CONTENTS

Preface / v

1
Making the Body Rhythmic / 7

2
The Teaching Environment / 16

3
Fundamentals of Rhythm in Movement / 38

4
Applications in the Studio / 84

5
Exploration of Compositions / 112

Afterword / 145

PREFACE

As the authors traveled about the country holding workshops in Dalcroze Eurhythmics, we came to recognize a genuine need. Participants in every workshop asked similar questions: "How can I take these wonderful experiences back to my private students when I don't have enough room in my studio to move about?" "I teach only one student at a time, not groups; how do I use Eurhythmics with only one?" We soon realized that teachers who work primarily one-on-one face a special challenge. During the workshops, these teachers could feel that body movement made music more alive and potent, but they needed help in taking the activities from large classes in generous spaces and revising them for single students in limited spaces.

Both authors engage in studio teaching as well as class and workshop teaching. In our studios we work one-on-one with our students, just like many other teachers, sometimes in a small space dominated by a large grand piano. Therefore, we have had to experiment with ways to translate Dalcroze principles from group work into one-on-one activities. We sought ways to articulate these principles while writing *The Rhythm Inside: Connecting Body, Mind, and Spirit through Music* (Alfred Publishing, 2003), in which we examine the physical systems that coordinate movement, thought, and human behavior. Through the process of understanding why Dalcroze exercises have certain effects on behavior, we have a basis for revising class activities to one-on-one teaching without losing the power and effectiveness of group work.

Many teachers who have participated in only a single Eurhythmics class return to their teaching with an urge to pass this experience on to their own students. Time and again people have called us to say, "I tried this idea with one of my students and it worked!" These teachers realized that changes came about in their students' playing in a way that felt like magic, and were convinced that music should be experienced away from an instrument. This is a major break with traditional teaching, which holds the tenet that "to learn to play an instrument, you should play an instrument." Instead, we should focus on the principle that what we are studying is Music itself; the instrument is the tool for bringing Music into our physical world of the senses. With this principle in mind, we can move our students away from their instrument without feeling that we are "wasting time." We are instead *gaining* time by getting to the essence, flow, and the impulse of music. When that is strong, technique will follow, not without practicing and concentration, of course, but with an awareness of the musical goal that the player is striving to achieve. The image of the music will urge the student into getting to the next beat so the pulse goes forward, or breathing so the phrase rises and falls with the same beautiful curve they have felt in their big muscles.

Although we include examples of our own use of Dalcroze principles, this is no recipe book. All students are different, all teaching situations are different, all teachers are different. This book addresses—and stresses—ways of responding to our students that are grounded in reliable Dalcroze procedures. In addition, by showing how flexible these activities can be, we seek to give teachers latitude in finding their own way to enhance this moment of music played by this student in this studio. The variety of possibilities is as great as the number of ways to play variations on "Twinkle, Twinkle, Little Star."

CHAPTER ONE

MAKING THE BODY RHYTHMIC

A budding composer in my Aural Skills class at Oberlin College came up to me after class and said, "You know, the best thing about the Eurhythmics we have done in class is that it has really helped my piano technique." I was quite surprised by his comment because I had not made any mention of the application of Eurhythmics to performance on an instrument. This experience, however, reinforced my own conviction about the value of Eurhythmics to performers: I recalled that I, too, had come to the same realization when I was a student.

How does Eurhythmics, which deals primarily with movements of the whole body, make such an impact on technique? The answer, as many insightful teachers have discovered, is that we play instruments with the whole body. Jaques-Dalcroze wrote:

> The fingers have to accent certain notes metrically or
> emotionally, to glide softly over certain keys, fingers
> and wrists must be alternately light and heavy, active
> and passive, subtle and rigid: and so the child should
> be capable of sensing throughout his whole body the
> many shades of intensity and touch.[1]

Famous piano teachers also realized that training the whole body was the key to superior performance. Abby Whiteside wrote:

> The body governs the fingers in playing the piano, and
> no amount of coaching in finger dexterity will ever lead
> to the easy beauty in playing that must be our objective.
> The fingers in themselves have no power of coordination.
> The body must be taught, and the fingers will find their
> way under the guidance of this central control.[2]

---

[1] Emile Jaques-Dalcroze, *Eurhythmics, Art and Education*, ed. Cynthia Cox, trans. Frederick Rothwell (New York: Arno Press, 1976), 122.

[2] Abby Whiteside, *Indispensables of Piano Playing and Mastering the Chopin Etudes and Other Essays*. (Portland: Amadeus Press, 1997), 4.

Thus we begin our "games" with exercises that involve the whole body in motion. It is the underlying movement of the body, which Whiteside calls the "basic rhythm," (we refer to it as the "fundamental gesture") that is the key to a flowing, thrilling performance. When we watch and hear a great pianist play, we are struck by the seeming incongruity of effortlessness combined with great emotional power and subtlety. This pairing is due to the fact that the whole body is coordinated toward a unified effect. While many people look at the fingers for a secret of how they "do it," the trained artist looks farther back, to the posture, the feet, the attitude of the head—the body is the instrument. Those who have seen Horowitz on stage remember that he seemed almost motionless as his fingers moved with great agility and speed. Sometimes, great artists make dramatic movements that involve the whole body and these moments are quite memorable. However, most of the time, the movement of the torso and upper body seems slight because the upper body acts as the controller for the split-second movements of the fingertips. Imagine someone cracking a long whip. A little movement of the wrist produces a surprisingly dramatic movement and loud sound at the tip. In the same way, even a small movement with the torso has great effect at the extremities.

When a player has learned to sense "the many shades of intensity and touch" throughout the whole body, the memory of these experiences leads to musical, as well as accurate, performance. The memory of how it felt to vary and control the energy flow in large muscles enables the small muscles (fingers, vocal folds) to respond in a coordinated effort. Then the movements at the instrument are flexible and expressive.

Gestures

When the whole body is coordinated in a concerted effort, we refer to it as the Fundamental Gesture. The music terms related to this physical expression are those of large-scale rhythm (phrase, period, and section) or form (exposition, development and recapitulation). Indeed, the Fundamental Gesture, defined in its broadest terms, refers to the concerted, focused and sustained movement of the body that develops throughout an entire piece. The opening exercises in Chapter Three, under the heading of "Tempo Variations" and "Dynamic Variations," focus on the whole body as a unified, rhythmic instrument. Attention to nuance is what helps us connect movements into coherent, expressive phrases. These studies serve as a foundation for all the exercises that follow.

Associative Gestures, which are the next level of movements in the hierarchy, involve primarily the muscles of the upper limbs. The equivalent music term is "rhythmic pattern," which is independent of meter and generally shorter in length than the phrase. It is important to understand that these Associative Gestures are connected to each other within the framework of the Fundamental Gesture. This is true, even with the smallest units of music, expressed by the smallest movements, which will be felt as gaining their integrity from the larger motions or background structure of the body.

Subsidiary Gestures are those related to the music term of meter (simple, compound, irregular, hemiola, transformation). We understand meter as a way of organizing beats within the gesture of the full-blown phrase, although phrase itself is not bound by measure's ever-present recurrence. Measures help shape the phrase, however, by accumulating tension and leading to relaxation. Their passage is a history of the specific composition. For instance, within a measure of music of the common practice period of Western music (1750-1900), the beats vary somewhat in timing, space, and energy, according to the qualities that we find at the level of phrase: there is preparation—anacrusis (beat 3 in 3-meter), initiation—crusis (beat 1 in 3-meter) and follow-through—metacrusis (beat 2 in 3-meter).

Within the Subsidiary Gestures, representing meter, are grouped the Subordinate Gestures, representing beat. These gestures are the domain of the smaller muscle groups at the extremities of our body. We can keep the beat with hands, fingers, feet and toes. This does not mean that the whole body cannot be involved in the movement for a beat; rather, the movements at the level of beat must be gathered into the larger levels of rhythm if the performance is to flow well. There is a danger, encouraged by many texts, of concentrating solely on beat, to the loss of a sense of phrase and larger gestures. Some students persist so diligently in vertical finger strokes that they find it very difficult to relieve their tension by involving larger muscles. Moreover, their concept of the flow of music resides at the finger-stroke level, instead of in the gesture that reaches out beyond the beats to the flow of the phrase. Giving the whole body the freedom of Fundamental Gesture keeps the "grand design" present in our consciousness, as we learn to cope with the Subordinate Gestures. (When we keep the beat with the whole body, we more readily feel its part in the flow of gestures which create musical performance.)

Finally, we refer to subdivisions of the beat as Supraficial Gestures. These are the music equivalents of the ornamentations that adorn Corinthian columns or the lace that adorns the table top. Although these gestures are less important to the overall structure of a piece, they are a vital aspect from the listener's perspective. Stravinsky remarked, after seeing a theoretical reduction of a familiar piece, "Where are all the notes that I love so well?" By using the term Supraficial, we intend to focus on the fact that control of these notes is governed by the larger muscle groups. As with beats, we can focus so intensely on the speed of the little notes that we develop musical, as well as physical, problems. The secret is to search for ways that our larger muscles can relieve the stress of quick movements. The result is to realize even more speed and brilliance than we thought possible.

The last exercises focus on counterpoint (polyrhythm, canon, fugue, ostinato forms, melody and accompaniment), which combines two or more lines of music, a basic requirement for pianists. In movement, this calls for different gestures in different parts of the body. Since our natural impulse is to move symmetrically, guided by commands from one mind, through one nervous system, we must develop the capacity to send different commands to different parts of the body. This can happen when the mind has a variety of motor memories to draw upon and has acquired the practice of noticing muscular sensation. Consequently, although the counterpoint exercises are more difficult than the single-line studies of rhythm, the ability to carry on two strands of music at the same time can be done.

As an example, we present a description of an actual lesson, illustrating the application of rhythmic gestures.

The Lesson

Stefan enters the studio and proudly states that he has found a piece by Brahms that he wishes to study. He has learned the "A" section of the Intermezzo, Opus 118, No. 2 in A major. This is a first lesson with me as a piano teacher; however, he has studied Eurhythmics with me for several months.

A Demonstration

"Please begin."

As he plays, it is clear that the piece speaks to him and through him. He dwells slightly on certain harmonies so that the music has a fluid and engaging quality. It is a joy to hear this piece played with such a fresh approach. Still, the piece is new and there are obvious passages in which he has not yet found his voice. Some of the phrases portray indecision about a climax. Further, although the bass and the harmonies are understood, the melody does not sing out.

"Would you show me your first phrase of music in *plastique*?"

(*Plastique* was the term used by Dalcroze to refer to "acting out" a piece of music in movement.) Stefan is familiar with the process. In the Eurhythmics class, we had been working on some of the techniques of how to realize music in movement. While the individual's personal interpretation is paramount, we had been working on expressing a panoply of rhythmic parameters: beat, meter, phrase, dynamics, counterpoint and so forth. Stefan remarked that he had already been working this way and wanted to discuss some of his ideas. He explained that the movement of the body seemed to be more circular than straight and that the starting position was off balance; the arms and torso turned slightly in the direction opposite to where the hips were directed.

"Please show me."

As he started to move to the piece, already committed to memory, he seemed to uncoil as if he were a flower blooming on a sped-up, time-lapse camera. The well-wrought harmonies were apparent in his movements. However, as the phrase went on, his legs seemed to "stutter" and the effect was one of aimlessness—a lack of decision about the phrase.

"Where is the phrase going?"

He replied that he had not completely decided, but he thought that he wanted to go to the E major harmony at the start of m. 4. This was further confirmation of what had been heard in the initial performance.

"Could you clarify that in your movement?"

Stefan began again; however, in addition to the "wound-up" start position, he leaned slightly in the direction he was going to travel. As he traveled through the phrase, there was slightly more sense of heading to the climax, depicted by a special "place" in the room. Stefan remarked that it had not quite worked; however, on a subsequent try, there was more urgency, so that the third measure had a sense of *accelerando* into the climax of measure 4. He balanced this alteration with a lovely *denouement* on the first beat of measure 4, as the arms floated downward.

"Now try the phrase on the piano."

Stefan returned to the piano and played the phrase with more clarity and direction; even the *accelerando* had found its way into the performance. Still, the melody did not rise above all the beautiful, sinewy arppeggios of which Brahms was so fond.

"Would you try the *plastique* again, but this time sing the melody as you move?"

After an initial stumbling, Stefan remarked that he was having trouble with the movement, because he felt that he had to satisfy his need to express the bass and harmonies with the lower part of his body and find some way to express the melody with the torso. Aha! He uncovered a secret; there has to be a counterpoint between the bass and the melody. In a sense, he had already unveiled this intuition when he had started with the torso and the hips out of kilter. Now, his intellect had connected with his kinesthetic sense—the comprehension in the joints—and he was able to verbalize what his body knew. Stefan made several attempts at singing and moving, trying to realize both worlds at the same time. Each time there was improvement, but the image was not quite strong enough yet. He was aware of what needed work and how to practice.

"Just for now, try moving in place while singing."

This time, Stefan crouched much lower and at the climax, his body was fully extended. The singing was also more comfortable.

"Play the phrase once again."

Now the melody was *en dehors* ("on the outside," Debussy would say), and the direction of the phrase was clearer. The tips of his fingers, playing the melody, had more life to them, as they "attached" themselves to the keys, rather than merely striking them. The piece was now taking on an element of depth (the high and low were in relief) and greater meaning, without losing the wonderful imaginative playing that he had demonstrated at the outset.

Discussion

This lesson was about allowing the student to find his own path to a way of expressing himself through the score. Of course, it is vital for the teacher to be prepared and know the possibilities of the score. However, if you look back at the teacher's comments (all in quotations), they are not directives to play a certain way; rather, they present ways for the student to explore, confirm, and modify his own musical voice.

Notice that the student's *plastique* revealed the strengths and weaknesses of the performance. The teacher may know what is "wrong" with the performance, but telling the student to "do it this way" or "that way" only builds up the sense that there is only one right way. A goal in teaching should be to foster independence in the student.

How has learning been encouraged here? Moving in *plastique* requires that the student maintain a sense of flow and focus. While he may not be thinking about every detail of the score as he moves, he has found a thread, perhaps the melody or the bass (both, in Stefan's realization), that compels him to continue moving.

If the piece has not been learned well, trying it out in *plastique* is a wonderful way to intensify learning and memory. Recall how Stefan moved to a "place" for the climax of the phrase. On repeated attempts, he moved to that same place in the room. The visual and proprioceptive sense of "place" for the phrase is another link for the mind to remember. There is a harmony there (an E major chord), which is linked to this motion. The emotion connected to that harmony is one of climax and then release. (Too often, in our attempts to help the student with a memory problem we will point out a harmony with its label, "V in the key of A." But this has little meaning in performance if it is not associated with the flow, place, and dynamic.) Further, the student has ownership of this phrase. In performance, he has something to say: "It is this type of movement to this place with this quality of expression." Having something to say is a powerful motivation to remember.

Our intent in this book is to help the studio teacher become aware of techniques from the Dalcroze discipline that can be useful in all areas of music learning. A secondary goal is to demonstrate how these techniques can be applied, even in a studio with limited space. In fact, the *plastique* was most successful at the end of the lesson when Stefan moved in place.

Some teachers may feel wary of having students move to a piece of music when they do not have experience with this approach. Nevertheless, trying out a *plastique* with a piece you are studying is a good place to begin. After working this way for a while, you will notice that your imagination grows tremendously. You will internalize the movements and then find that merely playing a passage conjures up the whole-body movement; your memory is strengthened and you have something to say through the music.

In my lifetime great pianists have abounded; some have used music to play the piano, and a few have used the piano to make music[3]

---

[3] Russell Sherman *Piano Pieces* (New York: North Point Press, 1997), 69.

CHAPTER TWO

THE TEACHING ENVIRONMENT

Before we go on to the descriptions of numerous Eurhythmics activities and their application, we need to help you envision the physical environment that facilitates this kind of teaching. With a clear picture of the studio, you will better understand and visualize the exercises that will be presented in Chapters Three, Four and Five.

In this chapter we demonstrate, through the use of Dalcroze "games,"[4] the ways in which props can be used.[5] These physical tools can intensify rhythmic feeling through both visual and kinesthetic sensations. Scarves, ropes, tennis balls, hand drums and other materials are valuable aids in experiencing different qualities of beat, pattern, phrase and larger gestures.

Since many teachers have a limited amount of space in their studio, we have designed the activities in the following chapters so they can be performed in a small area. It is highly desirable, if at all possible, to clear a space large enough for a walk or a short run.

Props for the Studio

Balancing the weight of the whole body moving in space—even a small space—tells us much about the flow of energy. We can bounce, roll, and throw balls; tap sticks; twirl scarves; and glide on our feet, in whatever way the music asks. The following pages list some of the instruments and activities that have worked well for us. Such a list is sure to be incomplete and open-ended. You never know what teaching situation will present you with an opportunity to pull something new out of the kitchen drawer. Be inventive, daring, even a bit crazy!

---

[4] The philosophy and application of these "games" that are essential to the Dalcroze approach are described in detail in Chapter Three .

[5] A teacher needs to try these activities before using them with a student. You must feel confident enough to carry on your own movements while monitoring your student's performance.

Rhythm-percussion

Hand drums, conga drums, bongos, or other drums

Claves, rhythm sticks, shakers

Triangles, finger cymbals

Balls (tennis, rubber, of various sizes for different ages and activities)

Rhythm-movement

Trampoline

Hoops

Pitch

Step bells

Xylophones and other barred instruments

Montessori tone bells

3-D Grand Staff

Dynamics

Scarves

Pillows

Feathers

Elastic exercise bands

Ribbons

Many of these items can function under several headings. Hand drums, instead of being tapped for beats, can be rubbed for a very soft sound without beats. This sound usually makes students think of snow or water, and the continuous, circular arm movement induces a feeling of long phrases and legato sounds. A triangle can be used to show the downbeat, but it can also show a difference in dynamics.

Rhythmic activities should be kept interesting and challenging by the introduction of variations, such as using other instruments and trading activities. For example: Without stopping the flow of the pulse, the teacher can call for a "change":

Student is ready to play her instrument.

Teacher stands near with a hand drum.

"Play any note in time with my drum beats."

"Ready, go."

Student plays one note on each drum beat, matching the teacher. (It is more interesting and musical if the pitch varies from beat to beat.)

"Play all the beats and count in groups of four."

Student continues playing all beats, while teacher taps only the downbeat.

"When I say 'Change,' play only on the downbeat."

"Change." ("Change" should be said on the fourth beat.)

Student plays only the downbeat, while teacher taps all the beats.

This pattern reverses several times.

The game of "change" appears in all Dalcroze work because of its effectiveness in maintaining attention. Human beings begin to lose interest in an activity after two repetitions and need some change, even a very small change, to refocus their attention. Establishing two "anythings"—high/low, loud/soft, gradually faster/gradually slower, forward/backward, right/left, quarter notes/eighth notes, I play/you play—sets up two ways of moving that can be practiced by changing at unpredictable moments. The call for "Change" must be timed so that it comes just before the moment of change and fits in musically with the flow of the pulse. The underlying tempo must continue uninterrupted. The general rule is to call the command ("Go," "Change," "Hup," etc.) on the beat before the action is to occur. Likewise, any other words spoken during an activity should be said or sung in a rhythmic way that maintains the beat and quality of sound desired: "now get LOUDER, GO! The goal is to strengthen the student's ability to think while playing, to maintain control over an activity that is changing during process.

Please consider the activities that follow as examples, not prescriptions. You can perform the same activity, using a different instrument from the list above or others devised by your own creativity. The important consideration is the suitability of the activity and the instrument in bringing the student and the music into closer contact.

RHYTHM-PERCUSSION

Hand Drums

Hand drums come in a variety of sizes, generally from eight to sixteen inches. Those with plastic heads are less expensive than those with leather heads, are easier to care for, and are very serviceable for both children and adults. I find ten- and twelve-inch drums satisfactory for a wide variety of activities.

The most intuitive use of the hand drum is to tap a steady beat or a rhythmic pattern. Start with the notion of pulling the sound out of the instrument, rather than merely striking the drumhead. This calls for a free arm movement, a bounce that lets the wrist respond flexibly, and brings the sensation of beat into the shoulder and back.

The drum strokes can be used to promote the student's sense of metric organization and to understand how a rhythmic pattern fits into a metrical structure. For instance, with the student standing, drum in hand, the teacher might say,

"Sway from side to side."

"Tap the drum at the end of each sway, as if throwing the music out into the room, first to one side, then to the other."

"When I say 'Hup,' tap two notes on the left sway and one on the right. When I say 'Hup' again, return to single taps on both sways."

This activity can be supported by the teacher at an instrument, playing to match what the student is doing, or by playing only the beat and giving the student the responsibility of feeling and performing the two-tap pattern. Such variations depend upon the teacher's judgement of what the student is capable of accomplishing. Begin with a simple activity, even with advanced students, and progress gradually into more complicated patterns. For some students, changing from one note on a beat to two requires concentration and practice!

Taps on the rim of the drum are quite different in sound from taps on the drumhead, and can be used to accentuate the sensation of meter.

Teacher and student stand facing one another, each with a drum.

Teacher begins tapping.

"Tap to match my beats."

"Now tap the rim."

"Tap head, rim, rim, head, rim, rim...."

"What meter do you hear?"

"3-meter, of course!"

Rhythmic patterns can be practiced with the contrasting sound of head and rim.

"Tap rim, rim, HEAD, with a strong thumb stroke on the head that lasts for 2 beats."

"Tap twice on the first 'rim' (eighth notes)."

This pattern of two-eighths-quarter on the rim, half note on the head, has grown out of the feeling for the beats established through musical repetition ("**Keep swaying**") and progression from simple to more complex.

Drums can be shared, teacher and student tapping alternate beats, or any number of other patterns:

Teacher sets tempo with four taps.

"**How many taps did I play?**"

With tempo and meter acknowledged, the teacher says,

"**Bend your knees slightly with each beat. Echo whatever I play.**"

Teacher plays 4 beats of rhythmic patterns she feels the student can copy successfully (one note on each beat is a good beginning, even with advanced students), then gradually challenges with slightly more complex patterns.

"**Now you be the leader.**"

This activity can lead to a specific rhythm in a composition needing rhythmic improvement or in preparation for sight-reading a new one.

Drawing imaginary shapes on the drumhead can help visual learners develop a reliable pulse.

"**With your finger, draw a shape (square, triangle) on the drum head.**"

"**Tap the corners of the shape over and over, while we sing the melody of your piece.**"

"**Bounce your knees on the beats.**"

Moving a finger along the visual shape helps establish a flow of movement in the arm, as well as in the musical mind. When well established, the flow carries over into the student's playing.

Rubbing a palm smoothly over the hand drum emits a "swishy" sound which can help to develop an arm freedom for legato, or can express a feeling of mystery or relaxation.

"Listen to the sound."

"Make the swish for a while, then change to finger taps. When you are ready, go back to the swish."

When the student decides the right time to change, this activity becomes an opportunity for improvisation. The two kinds of sound can even be attached to a story the student invents. If, however, the teacher determines when to go from one sound to the other, the swish and tap become effective sounds for a "Change" game.

Other types of drums can be used equally well for many of the activities you might devise. Try the bongos for the activities described above. Because the two drums are of different pitches, they lend themselves to musical arrangements.

The student sits on the floor, with the set of drums between her knees or tucked in one arm.

"Rock from side to side."

"Tap the bigger drum for one side, the little drum for the other."

"Tap 3 times on one drum, once on the other."

This is a simple pattern for establishing flow of beats; the taps on one drum can be changed to 2 or 4 or 5, depending upon what the teacher thinks the student can perform.

Patterns can become progressively more complex, but the basic flow from one side of the body to the other keeps the beats of equal size. At the same time, the different pitches of the bongos make the pattern even more memorable than on a hand drum.

These examples are simple indicators of what can be developed easily when you keep a drum nearby. Thirty seconds of concentration on the physical sensation of a rhythm and its relationship to the basic beat will save counting exercises which, even when accurate, are usually unmusical. Drums offer the chance to experiment with rhythms in ways that are delightful, instead of frustrating. Students and teachers can inspire each other to find musical ways to use these percussion instruments.

Finger Cymbals and Triangle

Because both of these instruments are made of metal, they have a ringing sound that lasts for several seconds.

The teacher stands, holding a triangle.

"Listen carefully when the triangle is struck."

"When the sound has disappeared, raise a hand."

This simple exercise requires very careful attention. I have yet to meet a student who isn't fascinated by the gradual disappearance of the sound. Because of their long sound, these two instruments often serve well as the downbeat.

"Play your piece, and I will play the finger cymbals on the downbeats."

This clear sound, occurring at regular intervals, can help an uncertain student become more aware of the length of the bars. The activity can be reversed: Teacher plays the instrument, student sounds the downbeat with the triangle or finger cymbals.

Finger cymbals are most easily played by holding their handles between thumb and forefinger, one in each hand, and moving them vertically past each other, so that the edges just touch in passing.

Claves and Rhythm Sticks

These instruments can be used instead of a hand drum in most activities. Light-weight rhythm sticks can be made from dowels, cut to 10- or 12-inch lengths and sanded at the ends. Different weights give different sounds, of course. You might want to have a variety.

Claves are played by laying one between the fingertips and the base of the thumb so that the palm makes an air chamber below. The other is the striker. Listen for a musical tone. If you play them like rhythm sticks by putting your hands around them, you will lose their lovely resonance.

Both instruments work well with a side-to-side sway of the whole body, as well as walking or stepping in place. They can be played in different positions: holding them low, close to the floor; to one side or the other; or high above the head. Moving from one position to the other, either suddenly or gradually, helps reinforce a sense of space in the flow of the music.

Teacher sits at the piano. Student stands nearby with rhythm sticks crossed, ready to play.

"Tap the sticks in time with my music."

Teacher improvises in simple style, keeping a steady beat.

"Stay with my tempo."

Teacher gradually increases tempo, then decreases, while student copies.

This is an exercise in attention, as well as an experience in feeling the push and relaxation of changes in tempo.

"Move your arms so that each tap is in a different location. Feel the music flow from one place to another through the space in between."

"Select four locations and follow the same route over and over."

Teacher plays in 4-meter, more slowly.

"Reach farther with your sticks as the beats become slower. Flow!"

Teacher increases the tempo.

"Your spaces are becoming smaller as you play a faster beat."

This exercise reveals the relationship of time, space and energy.

Claves and rhythm sticks can be used in rhythmic duets or canon between teacher and student. Such activities require focusing on acute listening, and they improve ensemble skills.

Shakers

Shakers can be purchased at a music shop or can be made by placing a few dried beans in the capped cylinder from photographic film. (Seal carefully with tape.) They are particular favorites with small children, because they fit the hand nicely and can be used with a relaxed, easy motion. However, since they make a two-part sound ("ka-chung"), they are not useful for precise rhythmic work. They do work well in a start-and-stop game.

"Shake your shaker when I do, and stop when I stop."

Teacher tries to catch the student off guard by stopping and starting at various time lengths, and the student tries to be alert to the moment of the teacher's stop. Adults, as well as children, can have their attention elevated by such an activity.

Shakers and swishes on the hand drum lend themselves to creative story-telling. Both can produce nonmetric sounds that paint an atmosphere, rather than beats.

Rhythm-Movement

Balls

Balls of various sizes, generally larger ones for small children, can be used for feeling the smooth flow of beats. Rolling a ball across the floor, while singing scale tones or a folk melody, helps develop a sensitivity to flow—to legato. It requires precise control to catch the ball, as well as to start the roll, but precise control never means tenseness. The movements must be made with the same smooth flow as the rolling of the ball.

Suppose your student is studying the opening movement of Beethoven's "Moonlight" Sonata and the three-note groups are sounding like single notes instead of a murmur.

"Come sit on the floor opposite me."

"I will roll the ball so that it reaches you in 2 slow beats (half-note beats)."

"You return it to me in 2 slow beats."

"Let's sing the melody as we go."

Teacher takes a breath or sings "and" on the upbeat.

Teacher rolls the ball to the student on the downbeat ("Roll").

Student returns the ball smoothly to the teacher.

This exercise not only induces the feeling of smooth rolls into the arms and wrists of the student, but promotes an awareness of the long flow from one bar to the next, and then on to the next, and so on, to the end of the piece.

Meter can be experienced by performing a series of ball bounces:

"Watch me as I bounce the ball and then catch."

"Say the words as I do the movement; 'bounce-catch.'"

"Copy my bouncing with your ball and continue saying 'bounce-catch.'"

"How many beats are we showing?"

"Of course. This is 2-meter."

"Now bounce with one hand, catch with the other, pass back to the first hand."

"Say 'bounce-catch-pass.'"

"Now we have how many beats? Yes, this is 3-meter."

"Try this one: 'bounce-catch-up-catch' for what meter? Yes, 4-meter."

"This one is harder. 'Bounce-catch-up-catch-pass.' How many? Yes, 5."

"Another way to show 5-meter is 'bounce-catch-pass-up-catch.'"

If there is enough room, these ball games can be expanded by walking, stepping on every beat, or stepping on the downbeat, or to increase the challenge, stepping only on '2,' for instance, or '2' and '4.' They can serve as preparation for sight-reading, as remedial work on a composition played with poor rhythm, or as a rhythmic foundation for games of manipulation and memory.

Ball exercises also focus the student's attention, strengthen mental control, and increase flexibility of rhythm. The following exercise is particularly effective, for instance, in promoting the student's ability to perform eighth notes easily on any beat.

"Bounce 4-meter. Say 'doo' on each beat."

"Now say 'doo-ba' on the fourth beat."

"Now on the third."

"Next, the second."

"And on the first."

"Now go through the series on your own, doing each one four times."

Trampoline

A small trampoline hides underneath my piano. It is often the first tool we bring out to help with rhythmic problems. Bouncing on the trampoline makes use of gravity and the rebound of the springs. The regularity of body sensation—up, down, up, down—helps students with poor rhythm feel the inevitability of the next beat.

While bouncing, students can clap or tap a drum on each bounce, on every other bounce, or in any of a myriad of patterns.

"Count your bounces in groups of three. One, two, three, one, two, three…."

"Clap on every bounce."

"Clap only on '1.'"

"Clap '1' and '3.'"

"Make the '1' clap into a big circle that lasts for two bounces."

"Be sure '3' is a smaller circle."

Establishing a reliable 3-beat pattern on the trampoline has prevented many a minuet from being performed in 4-meter!

Performance of subdivisions of the beat is improved by the awareness of the approaching next beat. Two eighths or triplets develop a relationship to the beat itself. Here is a challenging game:

"Tap the drum on each bounce."

"Tap twice on each bounce."

"Tap a triplet on each bounce."

"When I call 'Change,' go to two taps."

"When I call 'Change,' go back to three."

As the student goes back and forth between two taps on a bounce and three, he feels the push of a triplet after several beats of eighths (as in Chopin's Waltz, Op. 69, No. 1, in A-flat), and the restraint necessary when going from three eighths to a duplet (as in Debussy's "Clair de lune").

Hoops

Hoops come in several sizes. A 33-inch hoop will fit an average adult, but a 20-inch will do for a small child. Hoops can be used to mark a place for many activities:

1. Ear training

"While I play minor thirds, stand inside the hoop and clap the beat."

"When I change to major thirds, jump outside and step the beat."

2. Crescendo/diminuendo

"Sit inside the hoop; curl down as far as possible."

"When you hear my music make a crescendo, gradually uncurl and open your arms."

"When you hear a diminuendo, gradually curl down again."

3. Phrases

"I'll hold the hoop with one hand; you hold the other side."

"Stretch away from each other and come back."

"Let's do that again, with a slow count of four away and four back."

4. Anacrusis

> "We'll roll the hoop back and forth. Prepare with a back swing move and then the forward roll."

> "Say 'and' on the back swing and 'roll' on the forward."

5. Compound meter

> "Use both hands to hold your hoop over your head."

> "Listen to my music (Mendelssohn's "Venetian Boat Song") and sway from side to side."

> "Sing along with the melody."

Pitch

Step Bells

Small metal bars, pitched from a low C to the C one octave higher, are fastened to a wooden frame, built like stairsteps, with a leg underneath, supporting the higher end. The steps of the wood frame are cut carefully, so that the half-steps, E-F and B-C, are only half the height of the other steps. Students can see the rise of the steps and hear the rise of the pitches at the same time. Since some beginning piano students, including adults, find it difficult to relate the concept of musical up and down to a horizontal keyboard, playing step bells can reinforce the sound and sight connection. Placing the bells parallel to the keyboard can then help transfer their understanding of which way is up or down.

Young students, in particular, like to play tunes they know on the step bells. Time spent with the bells often helps the lesson become more musical. The physical freedom of using mallets, instead of specific fingers, helps the young student play in good rhythm. The visual information also prepares the student to know when to play the "next-door note" and when to skip over a note. All these observations carry over to instrument performance.

Step bells can also be used for rhythmic improvisation.

"Keep playing C-G-G while I improvise a melody."

"Play either high C or low C in time with my notes."

"I will play different C's, while you play any notes you want on the step bells. Be sure we stay together on the beats."

Time spent away from the keyboard pays great rewards. Singing and moving with musical flow (as with arms playing step bells) give the student a lively musical memory (physical, aural, and mental). This memory stimulates and guides the fingers for improved instrumental performance.

Xylophones and Other Barred Instruments

The principal difference between step bells and xylophones and other barred instruments is the physical shape of the instrument. Xylophones, like the piano keyboard, are horizontal. Their bars, unlike the piano keys, become smaller and smaller from left to right as the pitches go higher, giving the student a visual clue about pitch and direction. The association of pitch and direction will carry over to the piano and will help the student know "which way is up." This design makes them an effective transition instrument between step bells and the piano.

Montessori Tone Bells

These bells are manufactured to match each other in appearance. Their only difference is their pitch. Students must listen carefully to arrange them in a scale, for instance, or a triad pattern, or a melody. They must know "which way is up" by ear only—no more visual cues, as with the step bells and xylophones—and can set them along a shelf or a table in the proper pitch order. They can be used for rhythmic improvisation:

"Arrange the bells in scale order."

"Set one bell at the left side and tap it as the downbeat in 3-meter."

"Use your right mallet to play the others on the remaining beats."

"Experiment with repeated notes and changing notes."

repeated notes

changing notes

"Experiment with different rhythms: quarter-two eighths-quarter."

"Play the melody from one of your pieces."

Wooden Grand Staff

I first saw a five-line staff made of dowels and uprights in a friend's studio some years ago. I was convinced immediately that the physical motion of grasping the line and naming it would make a much more profound impression than looking at a note on a page or even tapping notes on a chart. In piano study, of course, we must learn the full Grand Staff.  Therefore, I had a double set of staves made, with independent links at the side so that we can work with only one staff on some occasions and quickly reassemble it as the Grand staff. A separate short dowel is hung between the two staves for middle C. (We call it "Swinging C.") A set of lines and spaces which can be touched does indeed generate a strong feeling of place.

"Grab swinging C. Now grab each bar going up and say the name."

"What intervals were you showing? Yes, they are all thirds."

"Grab the very bottom line. What clef are you in? Yes, that is the bass clef."

"Come up all the bass lines, saying the names."

"Name the spaces going down. Put your hand out flat between the lines."

Teacher can set a metronome at whatever speed is suitable for the student:

"Name line-space-line-space from bottom to top—all 11 lines, 10 spaces."

"Now name them back down."

This last activity can be divided between teacher and student, one naming spaces, one naming lines. The staff can be used to locate the notes of a melody while it is being sung. More applications are described in Chapter Four under SIGHT-READING.

Dynamics

Scarves

The fluid quality of a scarf helps students feel the flowing characteristic of music. Be sure you find scarves that will make graceful curves. Always test fabrics and scarves for fluidity. Most synthetics are too stiff to swish satisfactorily. The scarves must be large enough to draw a legato line in the air. Handkerchief size is too small.

The teacher must observe the student's movement and be sure that the wrist is supple enough to lead the scarf through curves and circles. The student's knees also should be flexible, so that the whole body weight contributes to the sway.

"Bring the scarf horizontally across your body. Swish right, then left, slowly." (Each swish is a bar.)

"With your wrist, make the scarf dip for each beat."

(Teacher adds beats with a steady and clear downbeat.)

"Always put beat 1 on the left side."

"Come back quickly to the downbeat."

This pattern emphasizes the crusis (downbeat) and the energy of the anacrusis. The resulting swoop connects the end of one bar and the beginning of the next.

"Now let's do these motions to some music."

"Sing the melody of your piece and feel it float with the scarf."

A scarf is an excellent medium for feeling a rubato passage. Consider the *delicatissimo* passages in the Chopin Nocturne in A-flat, Op. 32, No. 2. Tossing the scarf up in the air and sensing the *rallentando* of the descent can help a student accomplish a more sensitive performance of rhythmic nuance.

Pillows

A pillow seems an unlikely addition to our musical props, but it can serve very effectively in several situations, especially for piano technique. A small (10" x 10") pillow is sufficient.

"Put your hands on the pillow."

Teacher has placed the pillow over the closed fall board or on a table.

"Push into the pillow with the heels of both hands and then pull out by lifting your wrists."

"Repeat this movement, feeling the 2-beat motif."

"Play your Mozart Theme (Sonata in D, 3rd movement, K. 284) and use this movement for the push-lift pattern in bars 8 and 15."

Mozart, Sonata in D, K. 284

Bar 7

Bar 14

This specific wrist movement is used on the piano to achieve the contrast in energy of the two-note motif. While this movement may not be part of another instrument's technique, the sensation of the energy flow is the same. When experienced with the back and arms, the feeling goes into the body's memory and guides musical performance on other instruments.

Feathers

Feathers, like scarves, must be tested for "floatability." Feathers can be blown, pushed up by a shoulder or hip, lifted with the back of the hand, and kept up in the air by any number of other motions. When the rule of the game is to move the feather upward on each beat, no matter where it has floated to, the body executes some wonderful contortions! However, the whole exercise is a study in rhythmic continuity. Transferred to an instrument, the memory of the movements becomes a basis for the extended flow of a whole composition—keeping the musical "feather" afloat.

Elastic Exercise Bands

Many gym-equipment catalogs include various items that are used for stretching exercises. Two of these can serve as a means to develop a sense of the long phrase.

Teacher and student stand several feet apart, facing in opposite directions, side-to-side (not back-to-back), each holding an end of a single band. Student is learning Prelude IV in C-sharp minor, from the *Well-Tempered Clavier*, Bk. I in which the first measure is echoed by the second, the third by the fourth, and so on. The tempo is slow; the movement is curved.

"Sing the melody and lean away from me during the first bar."

"Slowly come back toward me, while singing the second bar."

The smoothness of the pull and relaxation (the latter is harder to control) conveys a feeling of length and continuity which is often missing from a composition with long lines.

Ribbons

Ribbons (about three feet long, three to four inches wide—it varies with students of different size), attached to a small dowel (about 12 inches long), require free arm movements from the shoulder. Students may use one, switching from hand to hand occasionally, to exercise both sides of the body. With one in each hand, long, continuous sweeps can be made, one arm circling up, as the other comes down. As with the scarves, the movement of the ribbons can arouse a sense of flow. Ribbons are useful in a range of speeds. Experimenting will show you the limits—too fast to convey a music feeling, too slow to move the ribbon with graceful curves. (Music to accompany this movement can be glissandos played up or down the keyboard by the teacher or compositions with arpeggios, such as Chopin Etudes, Op. 10, No. 1, or Op. 25, No. 12.)

All of the props and suggestions described here express one basic idea: the music itself is the goal; the instrument is the means of getting there. Too often, we lose the music in being concerned with the instrument. Time spent in movement activities, away from the instrument, should be seen as an efficient learning mode, getting straight to the heart of musical expression and yielding great dividends in musical performance and appreciation.

> *One does not wish to dismiss the legitimate preoccupation with technical facility—as long as it truly facilitates and serves music. For technique is much more than a bill of particulars; it is the infinitely sensitive, fluent and faithful means of rendering the composition's form and field. Technique is a retinue of beasts and battalions commandeered by the imagination for the service to the Muse.[6]*

---

[6] Russell Sherman, *Piano Pieces`* (New York: North Point Press, 1997), 40.

Chapter Three

Fundamentals of Rhythm in Movement

The Dalcroze method embraces a philosophy of education that is student-centered; the focus is on the gradual development of the student's musicality, not simply the learning of literature. Consequently, the teacher must be sensitive to the developmental level of the student at any particular moment. While we give you examples that you may try, you may find that part of an activity as described may have to be repeated or altered to fit your student's momentary need. It may not even be feasible to get to the end of an exercise on some occasions. Your own personal and musical sensitivity will guide you in reshaping these examples to suit the moment.

A Dalcroze exercise is like a music performance: there is preparation, a decided beginning, and a rhythmic continuity that obtains throughout. At its best, the lesson itself is a thrilling music improvisation, where the teacher and student ride on and contribute to an underlying rhythm (Fundamental Gesture), which brings the student's body, mind and spirit into communication. Eurhythmics is a way of experiencing and exploring musical sensation and musical knowledge together. Progress begins the first time you walk through the music with your feet, instead of your fingers.

The exercises in this chapter are based on an educational philosophy developed by Jaques-Dalcroze, in collaboration with the eminent psychologist Eduoard Claparede. Their concern was to improve the quality of music education and education in general, by finding ways to increase the capacity for learning. Their experiments convinced them that the central necessity was to elevate the levels of attention, concentration, and memory in Dalcroze's students. They devised a set of "games" to accomplish these goals: exercises in the form of "Follow," "Quick Reaction,"

"Replacement," and "Canon." You will notice references to these games, as we discuss the specific exercises.

In the "Follow" game, the teacher plays "follow the leader," by demonstrating a movement, or performing a pattern, or changing dynamics, while singing a tune; the student-follower must imitate the teacher's activity, paying close attention to every change. The leader challenges the follower by varying patterns, movements, tempo and so on, at unexpected moments. Throughout these exercises, the element of "change" becomes the key to challenging the student's attention and concentration. For example, in Exercise 3.2, *Accelerando and Ritardando*, the student follows the tempo of the music, as the teacher increases or decreases the speed of her performance.

In the "Quick Reaction" game, the student continues repeating a pattern until a signal given verbally or by a musical cue tells the student to change to another activity as quickly as possible. For instance, in Exercise 3.1, *Sound and Silence (Start and Stop)*, the student continues to move to the music until the teacher stops playing, at which point the student must stop immediately. The basic pattern of the game is to develop any two or more activities which the student must be ready to execute at a signal.

The "Replacement" game involves substituting one activity for another when the teacher gives a command. For example, in Exercise 3.21, *Subdivision*, the teacher asks the student to replace a single tap for a beat with two taps. By varying which beat in the bar is to be altered, the teacher can vary the difficulty of the exercise. Replacement can also be done by setting a pattern: A triplet is performed on beat 4, on beat 3 in the next bar, then on beat 2, and finally on beat 1 without any commands from the teacher. This develops memory, as well as physical control.

"Canons" are the most challenging games; the student is asked to repeat a pattern after a pause in time. In Exercise 3.22, *Subdivision*, the teacher begins with an interrupted canon, saying, "Repeat what I do, 2 beats after me." The teacher listens and watches while the student performs, and then gives 2 new beats. The more advanced the student, the more beats the teacher can give and the more complex they can be. After some experience with "Interrupted Canon," the teacher increases the difficulty of the exercise by saying, "I will play without stopping. Continue to follow me at a 2-beat interval." The student must perform and, at the same time, listen ahead to the new pattern. Dalcroze refers to this as "True Canon," or "Continuous Canon."

Exercises

In building the performance of a music composition, (this applies to eight-bar beginners' pieces, as well as Chopin Ballades), we must begin with the overarching shape of the Fundamental Gesture. Proceeding this way, we can always sense the relationship of the details to the whole and develop an understanding of their relative importance and function.

This chapter presents activities that focus on successively smaller and smaller parts of the musical scheme. From the Fundamental Gesture to Supraficial Gesture, the exercises explore all the levels of awareness, understanding and control we must develop on the way to expressive music performance. Although most of the exercises include specific compositions to illustrate the activities, teachers will see how these activities can be used to approach similar compositions. In addition, there are limitless variations teachers can devise with their own students for the same musical purpose.

Throughout the exercises, we have been careful to use commands (in quotation marks and bold) of as few words as possible, primarily because most people hear only a few significant words of any set of directions. The teacher wants to help the student develop a decided sense of confidence at the outset. Fewer words allow the teacher to express clearly what is most important. Each exercise proceeds to more and more difficult variations, so that the student is not allowed to lapse into automatic movement. We need the student's attention to ensure as much growth as possible, but the progression must be by simple steps, or it will overload the student's capacity and prove detrimental to the rhythm of the lesson.

At the end of the activity, under the heading "Reflections," we have made suggestions in the form of statements and questions. Reading the questions before doing the activity can help guide your observations during the exercise. Throughout the activity, an underlying rhythm should be maintained; therefore, we have indicated special times at which some of the commands should actually be delivered—sometimes, on which specific part of the beat. However, because so much is dependent on the interaction of the teacher and student, there is no way to map out a Dalcroze lesson exactly. Therefore, these lessons, at best, can be only guides. You must be the experimenter.

Although some of these exercises are beyond the level of young students, none is too simple for more advanced students. You will speak differently to students of different ages, whether adult or adolescent or first-grader, but none should be denied the benefit of the simplest exercises. Older students often need more help than younger ones to open themselves to the flow of music. Focusing the mind is a skill that requires renewal throughout life.

We begin the exercise section of this book with a description of the "Preparation," known as "ready position." (Think of the moment when conductors reach the podium and lift their arms to command the attention of the orchestra. The performers must be in "ready position," or the music will not begin successfully.) The teacher then issues commands, by music or speech, that invite the start of the activity. It is important that the tone, dynamics, and timing of the commands be appropriate for the music about to be performed. Imagine what would happen to an orchestra whose conductor made a quick, vigorous gesture as the anacrusis to Beethoven's Allegretto movement in Symphony No. 7, or Debussy's "*L'après-midi d'un faun*"!

Warm-up
Sound and Silence (Start and Stop)

Exercise 3.1

Objective:

This simple "Quick Reaction" game involves only the contrast between movement and non-movement. (Conscious action and inhibition establish basic self-control and awareness.) The "Start and Stop" game induces a state of alertness that can establish a good "tone" for the lesson, or it can be used to revive alertness when attention flags. It can be done at the very first lesson. It emphasizes listening with great concentration, which is absolutely essential in performance at any level. It also establishes an atmosphere of fun and challenge. "Start and Stop" raises the level of attention quickly and without words; the music itself is the means of communicating.

READY POSITION

Preparation for being alert begins with posture. The student's knees should be slightly bent and the body weight balanced, so that arms, torso and legs are free to move with flexibility.

Preparation:

T (Teacher) at piano, S (Student) standing

T plays *glissandi* up and down the keys (sometimes white, sometimes black).

"As long as you hear my music, let your arms swing."

"Lean side to side; sway like a tree in the wind!"

T still playing.

"Stop when the music stops."

T stops and watches to see how quickly S responds.

T begins again, varying the length of each period of sound.

Reflections:

Did you change the lengths of each period of music?

Did S stay physically poised, ready to move as soon as the sounds began?

Did S listen while moving, so as to stop quickly when the sound stopped?

Was S in balance at the stop?

Now that attention is focused, we are ready to proceed with an exploration of ways to enrich your students' experience of music. From Fundamental Gesture, which expresses the overarching flow of music and all its nuances, we go through Associative Gestures such as pattern; to Subsidiary, at the level of meter; Subordinate, dealing with beats; to Supraficial Gesture, focusing on the subdivision of beats.

Fundamental Gesture[7]
Tempo Variations

When composers indicate that players should slow the tempo (*ritard, ritardando, rallentando*) or that the tempo should increase (*accelerando, stringendo*), they are expecting these moments to stir a physical and emotional response in the listener. Because the underlying pulse of music is so critical to our perception of a composition, changes in tempi affect our sense of the underlying structure (Fundamental Gesture) of the work. Imagine the effect if a Chopin Nocturne were to end strictly in tempo, instead of tapering to a close; consider Brahms' *Hungarian Dances* played in strict tempo, without the colorful effects of rubato.

Shifts of tempi convey human emotions. Speeding up conveys

---

[7] Refer to Chapter One to review the explanation of the Gestures.

enthusiasm, anxiety, or fear, whereas slowing down evokes the feeling of sadness, tenderness, or tiredness. Dalcroze was fond of using walking as a means of experiencing changes in tempi and their related emotions. Imagine walking to the bus stop and seeing the bus arrive while you are still a half-block away. How do you move? What are your emotions? If you miss the bus, how do you move? What change takes place in your posture? Your feelings? In the same way, when we perform variations in tempi, we illustrate the movements and emotions that find their counterpart in our daily life activities. By reacting to the tempo variations with the whole body, we clarify the Fundamental Gesture and the emotions that are associated with it. This strengthens our performance, through a deeper connection to the music we are playing.

Accelerando and Ritardando

Exercise 3.2

Objective:

This game can be used to illustrate *accelerando* and *ritardando*.

Preparation:

T holds drum, S ready to step in place.

"Listen."

T plays steady beat.

"Step to the beat (can be done in place).**"**

T speeds up or slows down, S matches tempo with steps.

"Gradually go faster for 10 counts, slow down for 10. Count out loud."

"Go."

"Faster for eight, slower for 12. Count to yourself."

"Go."

Reflections:

Was S able to match your tempo changes?

Did you find your playing changed in dynamics, as well as tempo?

Did you speak instructions during movement, so the beat flow continued?

Try letting S step and play the drum.

Did you monitor the number of beats while S performed?

Exercise 3.3

Objective:

This exercise develops restraint in sustaining a long accelerando.

Preparation:

T ready to play "In the Hall of the Mountain King" by Grieg (may use a recording), S stands near piano, holding triangle in one hand, striker in the other.

"Listen."

T plays very slowly (suggestion: two melody notes = 66, accent on the first).

"Strike the triangle with my accents."

"Go." (spoken softly, one half-beat before beginning to play)

"Make a circle with your arm as it moves between strikes."

T continues through *accelerando*, until ready to stop.

"And stop." (said on last 2 beats)

Reflections:

Did S follow your tempo and dynamics?

Did the circles become smaller?

Was S's whole body involved?

Did you suggest "Bend the knees," to help keep the body flexible?

Variation:

S crouches as low as possible at the beginning,

"Slowly stretch higher and higher, for the whole piece."

S's hands are stretched above head by the end.

"Again, and this time, spiral up like a vine as you stretch."

Reflections:

Try enhancing the effect by having S trail a scarf in one hand.

Did S rise too quickly and find he needed to adjust the tempo of his movement to fill the space available, or too slowly and needed to hurry up?

Exercise 3.4

Objective:

The following exercise on the trampoline helps students feel a gradual change in tempo.

Preparation:

T at piano, S on trampoline.

"Bounce."

"Bounce higher."

"Higher."

"Keep knees slightly bent."

"Bounce lower."

T matches the bounces with chords or rhythmic patterns.

"Follow my beat."

T plays section of piece in which there is a *ritardando* and/or *accelerando*.

"And stop."

Reflections:

Were you able to maintain the *ritardando*?

Did you have to encourage S to go higher?

Did you adjust your playing to match the *ritardando* in S's bounces?

Variation:

"Show me a *ritardando* with your bounces, and I will play to match."

Reflections:

Did you follow the S's tempo closely?

Was the S's change gradual?

Rubato

Exercise 3.5

Objective:

Rubato is an emotional ebb and flow, a stretching or contraction of the beats. The small deviations from regularity, heightened by lifting a scarf into the air and watching its curve, give the Fundamental Gesture a similar moment of broadening.

Preparation:

T at piano, S holding a scarf.

"Make a figure eight in the air with your scarf."

T says "Bigger," or "Smaller," as preparation for the entrance of the music.

T plays to match S's scarf movements.

T introduces rubato moments.

S follows the tempo of the rubato.

"And stop."

Reflections:

What meter were you playing in to match the scarf?

Perform the exercise again, moving the scarf in various ways.

Do you play differently when the scarf makes different shapes?

Was the S's whole body involved in the movement?

Did you have to say, "Bend the knees"?

Were you both sensitive to the drag of the scarf at the moments of rubato?

You might use Stephen Heller's "At Evening," Op. 138, No. 14, for this exercise.

Dynamic variations

Crescendo and Diminuendo

Music has a second powerful way to affect our response: shifts in dynamics—*crescendo* and *diminuendo*—pull us along on their fluctuations of sound. They keep us focused on the underlying flow of music by changing our physical response, which in turn arouses our emotional response. Recall the prolonged *crescendo* of Ravel's "Bolero": stretched over the whole composition, it creates a tension which demands our attention. The excitement which comes from the increasing level of pressure in our ears spreads through our whole body. We can barely resist the urge to dance!

Abrupt changes, which we call accents, also have their genesis in our movements and emotions. Accent is a quick moment of stress, as in "making important." A leap, a sudden turn, a laugh, a yawn, a sneeze are all degrees of accents from human movement. In a piece of music, these sudden dynamic changes serve as points of importance in a phrase and help us guide the energy of the Gesture. Accents of different kinds–metric, agogic, textural, pattern–abound in music. We create them in performance through an increase in energy—in power—which comes from deep inside and pushes out to the extremities. The physical experience of increased pressure felt through the whole body prepares the student to express these nuances well.

Chopin's Prelude in E minor, Op. 28, No. 4, is an appropriate example. At the end of a lengthy phrase, there is the outburst of a passionate cry, with changes in both tempo (*stretto*) and dynamics (*forte*), which almost immediately subside through a *diminuendo* to the earlier level of soft tones. What feelings do soft tones evoke? Wonder, disquiet, tiredness, peacefulness, to mention a few. And loud? Have your student make suggestions. Act out scenarios, like catching the bus, to sense how body posture changes, the manner of moving, the degree of tension in the muscles.

Exercise 3.6

Objective:

This exercise involves the relationship between space and energy.

Preparation:

T at piano, S holds a rather heavy book or object with two hands.

"Swing the book from side to side."

T says "Bigger," and "Smaller," as preparation for the entrance of the music.

T plays accompaniment to match S's swings.

(Suggestion: Chopin's Cm Prelude, Op. 28, No. 20, MM = 56)

T plays *crescendi* and *diminuendi*, while S follows T's dynamics.

"And stop."

Variation:

Repeat the exercise, with S swaying an imaginary object.

(Recalling the feeling of the weight of the book internalizes the sensation by storing it in memory for later performance.)

Try the exercise with heavier or lighter objects.

Try the exercise with changes in tempo.

Reflections:

Did the student involve the whole body in the sways?

Did the student's knees remain flexible in the soft passages?

Did the student continue to move in the soft passages?

Accent

Exercise 3.7

Objective:

    The "feminine ending" of language rhythm exists in abundance in music. All *appoggiaturas* have an inherent tension and release which creates this "push-relax" sensation. Ss who are concentrating on reading note by note miss this nuance, which is vital to the flow of energy and the feeling of breath.

    (The next two exercises, like others in this book, refer specifically to work at the piano. Teachers of other instruments can alter them, without losing the connection from whole-body movement to non-finger movement to finger movement.)

Preparation:

    T and S face each other, palms upright, ready to touch

"Palms up and lean forward to touch."

"Push back gently."

"Lead with the wrists."

    T and S repeat several times (ca. MM. 50, one beat for "lean," one for "back").

"Faster now."

    T and S add nonsense syllables ("dee-um") to vocalize the movement.

    T moves to piano, plays *appoggiatura* figure in time with "dee-um."

"Come to the piano and play 'dee-um' on the music rack."

"Lead with the wrists."

"**Play fingers 2-3, 3-4, 2-4** (and so forth)."

"**Move fingers to the keyboard; play 2-3** (and so forth)."

"**And stop.**"

Reflections:

Did you feel S's weight?

If not, did you encourage S to lean into your hands with full weight?

Did S keep the flow of "lean-release" going after returning to piano?

Did the wrist carry a flexible connection through the arm to the whole body?

Was the second note softer than the first?

Were S's back and shoulders involved in the movement?

Did you use some other finger combinations?

Did you change syllables, for the sake of interest?

Variation:

T at piano, S stands at a table with a pillow lying on it.

"**Put your hands on the pillow and lean into it.**"

"**Pull back.**"

S repeats several times.

T plays a "lean-release" figure at same tempo as S.

T varies tempo and dynamics, while S adds syllables ("dee-um") to vocalize the movement.

"**Come to the piano and play 'dee-um' on the reading rack.**"

"Play fingers 2-3, 3-4, 2-4" (and so forth).

"Move fingers to the keyboard; play 2-3" (and so forth).

"And stop."

T and S can trade activities.

Combining Tempo and Dynamic Variations

Exercise 3.8

Objective:

People tend to generalize their energy response intuitively over both dynamics and speed. Generalizing energy is so common a behavior that we must consciously learn to use tempo independent of dynamic level. (Pitch level is a third element which complicates the equation of behavior even more.). When learning about *accelerando*, for instance, Ss should experience faster with softer, as well as faster with louder.

Preparation:

T and S face each other with hand drums.

"Watch, and then mirror what I do."

T holds drum low and to the side and begins tapping softly and slowly.

T moves drum diagonally upwards, while making an *accelerando* and *crescendo*.

"Your turn."

Continue exploring the other combinations of tempo and dynamics within the Fundamental Gesture of the diagonal drum movement:

accelerando with *diminuendo*;

ritardando with *diminuendo*;

ritardando with *crescendo*.

Reflections:

Did S match your gestures?

Did you and S share similar impressions of the gestures?

Discuss the emotional quality of these combinations.

Consider stories and characters which might suit each of the combinations.

Did you find that the different combinations caused you to move in different directions?

Variations:

T and S face each other, with palms touching.

"Touch gently and step slowly."

T and S step in place; steps becomes faster, pressure of palms becomes stronger.

"And stop."

T and S repeat with other combinations:

"Touch firmly and step slowly."

"Touch firmly and step quickly."

"Touch gently and step quickly."

Calling on the imagination ("like a hurrying mouse") is sometimes useful in coordinating tempo and dynamic variations;

asking students for images can help them elevate their own sensitivity to the physical and emotional impact.

Phrase

A coherent thought must begin, develop a sense of direction (meaning) and arrive at a sense of completeness.

> *Bonds of connection ought to exist between the movements of the body, "bridges" between their point of origin and their point of arrival, if they are to have an esthetic value and to convey emotion with suppleness and elasticity. In other words, periods of continuity and solidarity must be created in gesture.*[8]

Exercise 3.9

Objective:

The following exercise is designed to focus on the continuous movements of which Dalcroze speaks. We want to involve the whole body in what we call the Fundamental Gesture, so that the student will begin to comprehend that the body must work as a coordinated whole to achieve musical expression.

Long, sustained movements are not common in everyday life, because they are a physical challenge. Students often find these continuous movements to be difficult at first, as we model them through the Dalcroze technique called "Follow." Their delight increases when students begin to sense control over their body balance and the concurrent subtlety of nuance that they are able to portray with the smaller muscles.

---

[8] Jaques-Dalcroze, *Eurythmics, Art and Education*, 65.

Preparation:

T and S stand facing each other.

"Follow me."

T demonstrates Fundamental Gesture: feet parallel under hips (about a foot apart), knees slightly bent. (1) Bend at waist so that hands reach toward the floor (feel torso, head and arms as unified). (2) Rise from the floor through the legs and the muscles of the back, and lift the torso upward. (3) Let the right arm float up, as the follow-through of the upward rise. Bend down again and repeat steps 1-3, with the left arm floating. The body sways slightly with the shift of arms.

S repeats the gesture, alternating the right and left arms with the follow-through.

"Match your movement to the music you hear."

T plays slow *glissandi* up and down the keys (sometimes white, sometimes black) to guide the student's rise and return.

T varies lengths of *glissandi*, so that S must listen with full attention and change from one arm to the other at varying lengths of time.

T segues into singing or playing an ecclesiatical chant (example: "Veni Creator Spiritu"), or a similar asymmetrical melody, so that each phrase of the chant coordinates with the large Fundamental Gesture of the whole body.

"Let the arm follow the shape of the melody."

"And stop."

Repeat the chant.

"Sing the melody as you move."

"And stop."

Reflections:

Did S demonstrate a unified movement with the body?

Was S able to follow the shape of the melody within the larger gesture?

Could S recall the melody?

Did you encourage S to vary the movement?

Associative Gestures Pattern

Exercise 3.10

Objective:

The objective in this game is to develop a corporal understanding of rhythmic pattern. There are two steps to the process: to sense an underlying gesture which connects the segments of the pattern and to fit these parts appropriately into the space of the Fundamental Gesture.

This exercise begins with an "Interrupted Canon," so that the teacher can model the controlling gesture. As the lesson continues, the student is encouraged to vary his/her movements in response to the pattern.

Preparation:

T and S stand facing each other.

"Follow me, after four claps."

T demonstrates four claps, rising diagonally in front of the body (clap in circles with just the fingertips and concentrate on the spaces between the claps).

S follows, after four claps.

"one, one, One, ONE."

T demonstrates, while speaking the direction in *crescendo*.

"one—two taps—One—ONE."

T performs two claps in the time of one.

(For second note of the second beat, turn one hand to put back of hand into palm of the other.)

T performs two claps on each beat.

S imitates.

T returns to one clap per beat.

S imitates.

"Continue the pattern."

"When I say 'Change,' put 'two-taps' in the next beat."

"Change."

T speaks on the second half of the previous beat, so that S has time to react.

"And stop."

"I'm going to play a recording of a piece that uses this pattern."

T claps quarter—two eighths—quarter—quarter.

"When I say go, you perform the pattern, then wait while I perform."

T performs measure 1, S performs measure 2.

So that both can move, T plays a recording of Beethoven's Symphony No. 7/II. (Suggestion: Bernstein and New York Philharmonic.)

FUNDAMENTALS OF RHYTHM IN MOVEMENT | 59

T and S prepare to "converse" in movement, performing the pattern in alternation.

"Go!"

On the last of S's 4 beats: **"My turn."**

"Match your movements to the music."

"And stop."

(Due to the length of the excerpt, it may be advisable to stop before the A Major variation.)

Reflections:

Was S able to respond in a timely manner to the commands?

Was S showing the continuity of a Fundamental Gesture while performing the patterns?

Were you able to develop an expressive ensemble with S?

Variation:

Preparation:

T and S seated at the piano, both have a tennis ball in their right hand (We use a tennis ball, so that the student is freed from playing individual "right notes" to concentrate on the gesture of the pattern.)

"I'll use the tennis ball to play four sounds; you play four after me."

T plays four sounds on the keys, using the tennis ball, and controlling the movement with a single gesture of the torso and arm.

"Now you go."

S imitates the four sounds, maintaining the timing but varying the space on the keyboard and the energy.

T and S conduct a musical conversation, each responding to the other's nuance.

"And stop."

T adds two eighths on any of the four sounds, and S responds.

T speaks a new command while S is performing the previous example.

"You play alone. When I say 'Change,' put two notes in the next beat."

"Change."

T speaks on the second half of the beat, so that S has time to react.

"And stop."

Reflections:

Was your shift from two players to one smooth?

Did S respond to the changes in two-note pattern?

Did the two-note pattern flow into the following beat?

Subsidiary Gesture

Meter

> *Rhythm is an element of irrational nature. Metre exists and is maintained only through reasoning; it develops the powers of control. To vibrate without metre, then to express oneself with metre: such is the province of man and of the perfect artist.*[9]

---

[9] Jaques-Dalcroze, *Eurhythmics, Art and Education*, 54.

Meter arises from the patterns of regularity, such as in dance. These regularities permit us to apply measurements to the flow of rhythm. We call these measurements "meter" and rely on it heavily to express our musical gestures. Meter is the servant of music. Music subjected solely to meter is no longer music.

Exercise 3.11

Objective:

We begin our discovery of measure with an exercise that involves the regular patterns of a dance, such as a waltz.

Preparation:

T and S face each other, T models a waltz step.

T stands with feet together, moves right foot to the side (beat 1), slides the left foot over to the right foot (beat 2) and then lifts up on toes (beat 3) to prepare for the step back with the left foot.

"Say the movements: step–s-l-i-d-e–lift."

"Step with me."

"Continue while I play."

T at piano plays music for a waltz, incorporating changes in dynamics and tempo.

"And stop."

Variation:

Try these variations for other meters:

2-beat meter—step with R foot, lift L knee / step with L foot, lift R knee;

4-beat meter—step R foot (to the side), slide L / step R, lift L knee (reverse direction);

5-beat—4 small steps forward, knee lift / 4 steps back/knee lift.

(The knee lifts evoke a feeling of anacrusis, the build-up of energy that leads directly to crusis—the downbeat. This muscular experience helps students get over the barline and on to the next downbeat.)

Reflections:

Discuss the feeling of the different meters–happy, relaxed, bold.

Did S let arms move with the swing from side to side?

Did S keep head up, instead of looking at feet?

Metric Transformation

Exercise 3.12

Objective:

This exercise incorporates compound duple meter, simple triple meter, and their combination in metric transformation. Compound meter, with its three subdivisions, affects a curved beat, while simple meter, with two subdivisions, produces a straight beat.

The student is asked to show the beat in different parts of the body. The enjoyment of this game is increased by the addition of a tennis ball, which S bounces to match the beat of the music. To keep attention high, the teacher can include the game of "start and stop" ("quick reaction"), once the student demonstrates that he has mastered the ball bounce. This variation, which disrupts the automatic movements of "bounce-catch" that S has mastered, demands greater attention and concentration.

Preparation:

    Student standing, holding a tennis ball.

    "Listen."

    T plays the Rondo from Clementi's Sonatina in D, Op .36, No .6.

    "Show the beat in your knees; 1-2, 1-GO."

    T encourages a large gesture of the body.

    "Hips side-to-side… Shoulders sway."

    "Now bounce the ball."

    "Say, 'Bounce-catch.'"

    T says this in time with the dotted-quarter beat.

    T says "Go" on beat 2.

    S bounces on beat 1 of next bar, catches on 2, and continues.

    When this movement is well established, T adds 3-syllable sounds:

    "Lop-a-dee," "galloping," "all of us."

    T invites S to make up some more 3-syllable sounds, while continuing the bounce.

    "And stop."

    "Listen and follow me."

    T demonstrates 3-beat meter:

    beat 1, bounce with one hand;

    beat 2, catch with other hand;

    beat 3, transfer back to first hand, prepare for next bounce.

S imitates.

"Count with me, 'one—Two—THREE.'"

"Say 'Bounce-catch-pass.'"

"Listen."

T plays waltz or recording of waltz at moderate tempo. (Suggestion: Brahms', Waltz in A-flat, Op. 39, No. 15)

"Show the beat in your knees."

T encourages a Fundamental Gesture for the body.

"In your hips...In another place."

"Bend a knee when you hear beat 1."

"Ready to bounce?...Go!"

"And stop."

Variation:

(Metric transformation–more advanced.)

"Listen."

T plays Bernstein's "America" from *West Side Story*, Act I, Sc. T, No. 7, bar 50 and on.

"Bend a knee on beat 1."

"Clap lightly for all the eighth notes."

T demonstrates bounce combination of "bounce-catch," 2-beat meter (three eighths in each beat: "Ta-de-yah, Ta-de-yah") and "bounce-catch-pass," 3-beat meter (two eighths in each beat: "Tee-yah, Tee-yah, Tee-yah").

Eighth notes remain at a constant speed. Ball movements change: slower bounces in 2-meter, faster bounces in 3.

"Ready to bounce?" "Go!"

Student will discover a measure of 6/8, transformed to a measure of 3/4.

"When the music stops, you stop."

T introduces *accelerando/ritardando*, *rubato* and *crescendo/decrescendo*.

"And stop."

Variation:

"Bounce-catch for 2-beat meter."

"Take three steps (no bounce) for the 3-beat meter."

Reflections:

Did the eighth notes stay the same duration?

Did the student adjust easily to the changes of space necessary in the metric transformation?

SUBORDINATE GESTURE

Beat

"Beat" is the impulse—the "push"—to which we respond with toe-tapping or head-swaying or bending of the torso. Beat, according to Dalcroze, has three qualities: time, space, and energy. For instance, the regularity of walking, in which one side of the body is balanced first on one leg and then the other, makes walking an ideal expression for Dalcroze's description of beat. When we exert more energy, we can take longer steps in the same amount of time. If we maintain the energy level and take shorter steps, the timing speeds up. His development of Eurhythmics came from the realization that we carry in our bodies the means of creating and feeling the sensation of regular beats.

The following exercises are designed to help the student become aware that the whole body can express the beat. The ability to react physically to the beat is universal; however, it is easy to fall into inattention when reacting at the "toe-tapping" level. Therefore, we need to awaken the student to the multitude of ways that we can express the beat.

Exercise 3.13

Objective:

Exercise 3.1 was about moving and stopping; in other words, moving *while* the music was sounding. Now the game is moving *with* the music, moving to *match* the music. S is now ready to listen for the beat and move *with* it. This second level of attention arouses a feeling of moving with purpose, of being part of the music.

Exercise 3.13 focuses on preparation. At a signal from T, S should be physically ready, body poised for whatever activity is to take place. Even a small change in activity keeps S alert and involved, while the musical goal, repeated in many guises, is stored in memory. It must be remembered that stopping, just like starting, must be done *with ease and poised control.*

Preparation:

T at piano, S standing, ready to step (in place, if necessary).

"Listen."

T plays a melodic line (or chords) at a comfortable tempo (easy to walk).

"Step with each beat. When the beats stop, you stop."

If S is not matching the tempo, T changes playing to match S's steps.

T stops and starts. T can change tempo during or between playing.

"And stop."

T reverses activities.

"Stand while I play; walk when I stop."

T watches to be sure S walks in the same tempo.

"And stop."

Reflections:

Did S move with the beat?

Did you adjust the tempo of your playing to match S's steps?

Did you and S change tempo together?

Did you suggest other ways of moving to match the beat? (Try raising and lowering shoulders, jumping, hopping, clapping, tapping a drum.)

Did S move with a sense of always flowing to the next beat?

Did S stay in "ready position" during the stops?

Exercise 3.14

Objective:

This game begins with a "Follow," in which the student moves to the established beat. This captures the student's attention. The teacher quickly moves to a "Quick Response" exercise to develop the student's concentration.

Preparation:

> T with hand drum, (drum technique: pull the sound out of the drum with an arm gesture), S assumes a standing or seated position, as space allows "Ready position" for silent clapping (clap in circles with just the fingertips; concentrate on the spaces between the claps.)[10]

"Listen."

Teacher performs series of beats on the drum.

"Clap your hands to match the beat."

"Move your shoulders to the beat."

"Match the beat in one foot. In the other foot."

"In the head."

"In another place."

"Take a walk."

"And stop."

Reflections:

> Which movement seemed unfamiliar or awkward?
>
> Did some movements seem more appropriate than others for the beat?
>
> Was the student successful in matching movements to the beat?
>
> Variations: The teacher continues the exercise, but incorporates the following elements: *accelerando/ritardando, rubato* and *crescendo/diminuendo.*

---

[10]See Also: *The Rhythm Inside* p. 122

Exercise 3.15

Objective:

Joining voice with movement and music blends several ways of experiencing rhythmic beats. Speaking rhythmically and singing help pianists feel breath and phrasing. There are frequent opportunities to use the voice musically, even when speaking.

Preparation:

T and S face each other, T holding a tennis ball

T sets tempo by speaking a rhythmic phrase.

"Back and forth," or **"You and me."**

T begins the passing, S joins in the words and passes back to T.

T steps away.

"Pass between your own hands."

T goes to the piano and plays melody notes or chords to match the beat.

T and S can trade activities, giving S the chance to improvise.

T and S may want to use tennis balls for improvising at the keyboard

Reflections:

Did you vary this activity by speaking louder or softer?

Did you add footsteps to the beats?

You might sing a song or say a poem in time with the beats.

Exercise 3.16

Objective:

In this activity, S keeps the beat going when T drops out of the game. The activity can be tapping knees, passing an object (tennis ball, bean bag), saying a poem, walking, or swaying from side to side.

Preparation:

T and S hold a hand drum between them, or each has a drum

"Match my tap." (Both to move the drum through a large movement as they tap.)

Both tap at the same steady beat.

"When I stop, you continue."

T stops, S continues to play.

T re-enters and leaves several times, either to reset the beat or to change tempo.

"And stop."

Reflections:

Did S maintain flow of beats when T stopped?

Did S adjust to tempo changes?

Exercise 3.17

Objective:

Improvisation skills can be encouraged with simple activities. The give-and-take of improvising with another player requires an understanding of where the other person is in the music at all times.

FUNDAMENTALS OF RHYTHM IN MOVEMENT | 71

Preparation:

T and S both at the piano, with tennis balls in their right hands; T seated at the upper register, S at the lower

"When you hear this note, (T plays the highest note on the keyboard) I stop, you play."

T improvises by moving tennis ball across the keys or bouncing, sometimes on repeated notes. When T plays highest note, S begins to play.

"And stop."

"When you hit the lowest note, you stop, I play."

"Go."

S plays again. They go back and forth, as often as T feels is suitable.

"And stop."

Reflections:

Did S pick up the beat, dynamics, and musical character of your music?

Did you introduce some changes in dynamics and tempo?

Exercise 3.18

Objective:

The capacity to maintain an inner sense of pulse is valuable to any musician. Ss take great delight in this game's challenge to their concentration.

Preparation:

    T with drum, S standing nearby

    "Listen."

    T establishes a beat with drum or other instrument.

    "Put the beat in your knees."

    "Swing your arms."

    "Continue, no matter what I play!"

    T plays at a different tempo, or with no discernible beat.

    S strives to continue the original beat through all the distraction.

    T returns to the original beat.

    "And stop."

Reflections:

    Did S maintain a Fundamental Gesture (a flowing body movement) throughout?

    Did you use a blinking metronome or the second hand of a clock to be sure you returned to the same tempo after playing the distraction?

    Did S maintain the beat throughout the distraction and afterwards?

Exercise 3.19

Objective:

    This exercise uses the trampoline to help organize beats. When the beat sensation is well established, we can express stronger and weaker impulses, which result in measure groupings. The exhilarating bounce of the trampoline is an excellent experience of beats.

Preparation:

T at piano, S on trampoline.

S bounces, staying at the same energy level.

T plays single tones or chords to match the bounces.

T says, **"Count your bounces in groups of four."**

T should speak rhythmically, with the flow of the music.

After a short time, T says, **"Three."** (or five, seven, etc.)

S revises counting to **"One, two, three,"** without missing a bounce.

Reflections:

Did S make these changes within the flow of bounces?

Did you call the change a beat or half-beat early, so that S could keep the beat?

Variations:

"Clap on the downbeat."

"Clap on all beats."

"Clap on 1 and 3 and other beat combinations."

Reflections:

Did S clap musically, moving claps through vertical, diagonal, or horizontal space?

Did S's hands move in a circular motion between claps?

Did your playing match S's claps?

Variation:

>T at piano, S places hula hoop on floor.
>
>**"Put one foot inside the hula hoop, one outside."**
>
>**"Hop four times on the inside foot, four on the outside."**
>
>**"Go."** (T speaks on fourth beat before playing)
>
>T plays (improvises) in 4-meter.
>
>**"Hop 1 beat inside, 3 outside."**

Reflections:

>Did you change tempo and dynamics?
>
>Did S change energy in the movements to match?
>
>Try other meters.

Exercise 3.20

Objective:

>This game focuses on prolongation of beats. We approach the concept of longer notes through the physical sensation of "ties." For example, a quarter note-half note-quarter note can be interpreted as four quarter notes, where the second is tied to the third. This same procedure can be used for patterns within a beat. (A 16th-eighth-16th pattern can be interpreted as four 16ths, with the second tied to the third.)

Preparation:

>T and S with drums, S standing ready to step in place
>
>**"Listen."**
>
>T plays beats with drum.

"Tap to match my beat."

"Step in place to match the beat."

"Count the beats in groups of four."

"Step only on 1."

(Commands should be given so that the last word is on beat 4.)

T reminds S to show the length of the sound (4 beats, in this case) with the whole body, moving the drum horizontally, vertically, or on the diagonal.

"'1 and 3,' '1, 2 and 4,' and so forth."

T reminds S to show the space between the beats.

"And stop."

Reflections:

Did the student respond with the whole body to the prolonged notes?

Was there flexibility in the student's movements?

Supraficial Gesture

Subdivision

Exercise 3.21

Objective:

The objective of this game is to help S understand the space and energy adjustments required to divide the beat into 2, 3, 4, or 5 equal parts. T begins this game with an "Interrupted Canon," which lets S echo T's movement. T taps the drum in different places for the subdivisions and uses different fingers where the technique demands it.

Once these movements become confident, T introduces a "True Canon." "True Canon" means that T continues to play without interruption, while S continues to echo T's patterns at a certain number of beats behind. When more beats are added to T's statement, S faces greater challenges in concentration and attention to nuance.

Preparation:

T and S face each other, each holding a hand drum

"Follow me, 2 beats later."

T "passes" the beats to S, who passes them back. This is done within a Fundamental Gesture that gives direction to the beats, such as a sway to the left on beat 1, right on beat 2.

T divides either or both beats into 2, 3, 4, or 5 subdivisions and S imitates. (T ornaments a quarter-note melody, using: appoggiatura = eighth notes; mordent = triplet eighths; turn starting on the upper note = quadruplet 16ths; turn starting on principal note = quintuplet 16ths.)

Individual fingers may be essential for 4- and 5-part subdivisions, depending on the tempo.

"Continue to follow me, 2 beats later."

T and S develop a true canon.

"And stop."

T goes to piano.

"Tap the pattern 2 beats after me."

"Go!" (spoken on the second beat)

"Now 1 beat (or 3, 4, and so forth) **after me."**

"And stop."

Reflections:

    Did S follow the direction of your movements?

    Was S able to keep the beat while playing subdivisions?

Variation:

    S at piano

    "Play a melody in quarter notes at this tempo."

    T claps hands about. MM=60.

    "When I say 'Two,' play two eighths on the next beat only."

    "When I say 'Three,' play a triplet."

    "If I say 'Four,' play four 16ths."

    "If I say 'Five,' play quintuplet 16ths."

    "Now you choose where to add subdivisions."

    "And stop."

Variation:

    S at the piano, review terms *appoggiatura, mordent* and *turn*

    "Play a melody in quarter notes at this tempo."

    T claps hands about MM=60.

    "When I call out a term, play it on next beat."

    T calls the terms on the prior beat.

    "Now you choose where to add an ornament."

    "And stop."

Reflections:

    Did S maintain a supple wrist?

Did S release weight into the key (not push) on first note of the subdivision?

More advanced students may add a counterpoint below the melody.

Exercise 3.22

Objective:

Trampoline sets beat for feeling subdivisions in various simple or compound meters.

Preparation:

T at piano, S on trampoline, holding hand drum.

"Bounce in time to my music."

T plays steady beats.

"Tap the drum with every bounce."

"Tap twice for every bounce."

"Tap three times for every bounce."

T switches several times between saying "two," "three" and "one."

"And stop."

Variation:

"Bounce in time to my music."

T plays steady beats.

"Tap the drum with every bounce."

"Count your bounces in groups of four."

"Tap twice on 4."

T calls for two taps on varying beats.

T does the same with subdivisions of 3, 4, and so forth.

T changes the number of beats.

T plays a pattern from S's literature (eighth and two 16ths, for instance) and makes the connection between the exercise and S's music.

Concurrent Gesture

Counterpoint

polyrhythmics, canon, fugue

> *There is another important reason why, for the rhythmic training of man, it is necessary to exercise all his limbs, and that is—that a child is rarely born polyrhythmic. To create in him the sense of simultaneous rhythms, it is indispensable that he should be made to execute, by means of different limbs, movements representing different durations of time.*[11]

Exercise 3.23

Objective:

The goal with this game is to be as expressive as possible with two simultaneous lines of music. This training is especially important for the performance of music from the Baroque period, but the skill is necessary for practically all music that the pianist performs. We approach the problem by first acquiring skill with both parts individually and then combining them. A certain degree of automatic response with each of the two lines allows the performer to switch concentration from one line to the other.

---

[11] Emile Jaques-Dalcroze, *Rhythm, Music and Education*, trans. Harold F. Rubenstein (Aylesbury, Great Britian: Hazell, Watson and Vinney Ltd., 1973), 43.

The game begins with a "Follow," so that the student can become immediately comfortable with each of the parts. When the teacher is sure the student has control of the two patterns, they play opposing parts simultaneously. The next step is for the student to perform both lines simultaneously. The teacher should make sure that the student is secure with the drum taps before proceeding. This movement should display a degree of automatism. The student should be using the larger muscles to incorporate the three taps into a single group. This will further help the student make the pattern automatic.

The greatest challenge of this exercise is developing the ability to switch the roles of speech and the hands in a "Quick Reaction" game. At first, it is advisable for the teacher to demand the "switch" at regular intervals, until there is some level of success. When this has been achieved, the teacher can give the commands at random intervals.

Preparation:

> T and S face each other with drums (silent clapping may be used in place of drumming)

"Follow me, one bar later."

> T intones a 6-beat pattern out loud, while tapping on 1 and 4. (Silly syllables help: "Dig-a-de Dig-a-de")

> T taps 1 and 4 at two different places on the drum, maintaining a flowing movement in the body.

> T stops, S imitates ("interrupted canon").

> T continues pattern several times.

"And stop."

"Follow me, one bar later."

> T intones a 6-beat pattern out loud, while tapping on 1, 3, and 5. ("Dig-a Dig-a Dig-a")

T strikes three different places on the drum, maintaining the flow.

T stops, S imitates, while counting out loud ("interrupted canon").

T continues pattern several times.

"Maintain this pattern while I change."

Teacher returns to first pattern.

"When I say 'Change,' change to my pattern." (T calls "Change" at regular and then irregular intervals.)

"And stop."

"Listen."

Teacher improvises a waltz accompaniment with a duple melody (two dotted quarters in 3/4). The same musical pattern is found in Chopin's Waltz in A-flat, Op. 42.

"Tap the left-hand pattern on the drum."

"Count out loud on 1, 3 and 5."

"When I say 'Change,' tap the rhythm of the melody."

"Count on 1 and 4."

T calls "change" at regular and then irregular intervals.

"Keep tapping the drum on 1, 3 and 5."

"Count on 1 and 4."

"When I say, 'Switch,' reverse roles."

"You decide when to switch."

"And stop."

Preparation:

T and S seated at the piano, T plays ostinato in 6/8. Tennis balls may be used, or a composition such as Bartók's *Mikrokosmos V*, "Boating."

"Play any black key on counts 1, 3 and 5."

T counts 1-2-3-4-5-6, while playing the ostinato which clarifies 6/8 meter.

"Go."

T speaks "go" on count 5.

"When I say, 'Change,' play on counts 1 and 4."

"Change."

T calls "change" at regular and then irregular intervals.

"And stop."

"You play the ostinato."

"Add a melody on counts 1 and 4."

"When I say 'Change,' play on counts 1, 3 and 5."

"Change."

T calls "change" at regular and then irregular intervals.

"And stop."

T says, **"White"** or **"Black,"** to switch S's melody back and forth from white keys to black.

T says, **"Switch hands,"** to reverse activities of RH and LH.

S is now performing two meters simultaneously.

The organization of this chapter emphasizes the importance of the hierarchy of musical levels. The large Fundamental Gesture should underlie the concentration on every level, all the way to Supraficial Gestures. This approach is helpful at all stages of accomplishment. A beginning student should be as aware of the flow from the first bar to the second to the third and on to the last as the performer of a Brahms Intermezzo. The purpose of playing one note after another is not just to play one note after another, but to make music. The emphasis on knowing the sense of the music from the largest gesture to the smallest detail directs everyone's attention—teacher and student—to the MUSIC aspect of the MUSIC LESSON.

Chapter Four

Applications in the Studio

In this chapter, we give several examples of how Eurhythmics can play a key role in an actual lesson. We have organized these lessons under headings that are often used in traditional methods texts: Teaching Rhythm, Teaching Technique, Teaching Music Reading, Teaching Ear Training, and Teaching How to Memorize. Thus, the reader will see how Eurhythmics can be used successfully in each of these areas.

Eurhythmics, according to its originator, Jaques-Dalcroze, involved a three-part study of music: rhythmic movement, solfege, and improvisation, all of which we call upon to enhance a lesson. Dalcroze himself held improvisation as the goal of Eurhythmics, fostered by the musicianship developed in rhythmic movement and solfege. Historically, improvisation was a requirement of pianists for centuries and played a significant role in the teaching of instrumental playing. Dalcroze himself, studying at the Geneva Conservatory under the tutelage of Adolph Prosnitz, was required to be able to improvise in the style of composers whose works he was studying.

A Short History of the Piano Lesson

The model for the piano lesson is intrinsically linked to the rise of the piano as a performing instrument. Until the 1820s, the piano and its predecessor, the harpsichord, served as an accompanying instrument, either as part of an ensemble or to accompany soloists, most often vocalists. However, on occasion, pianists were included on concerts as "novelty" acts. In this regard, their chief function was to dazzle the audience with technical feats. Often, they would take familiar opera melodies as a basis for improvised bravura variations.

By the middle of the 19th century, the convergence of a number of factors led to the piano as the dominant solo instrument. With the rise of the middle class, families were able to afford pianos in their homes. Piano manufacturers, such as Pleyel, Erard, Broadwood and others, were able to market smaller upright pianos that were more suitable for the size of modest rooms in these dwellings. It became a mark of distinction for a member of the bourgeoisie not only to own a piano, but also to hire a teacher. Piano lessons were especially important for young women seeking positions of employment, because they were considered more marketable if they could list music as one of their accomplishments.

Virtuoso pianists, such as Liszt, Thalberg, Moscheles, and Kalkbrenner, captured the imagination of the public with their feats of technical wizardry, so much so that students flocked to them and their understudies, hoping to acquire these skills. Piano teachers in general were able to make a fairly good living by teaching alone, and even more, if they could establish themselves as virtuosi.

Sadly, the focus of training on the piano at this period was on acquiring technical facility as an end in itself, rather than seeking a deeper and committed expression of music. One need only peruse the quality of music being published for the piano at the time in order to comprehend the music tastes of the day. Carl Czerny, Beethoven's famous student, had achieved Opus 1000 by the time of his death; yet, apart from his Studies, his music is rarely played and even more rarely performed. His *oeuvre* is simply too trite for the serious classical-music enthusiast. So voracious was the public in his day for the keys to technique that charlatans were able to sell bizarre mechanical contraptions that laid claim to producing astonishing piano dexterity without the use of a piano! For example, one such device involved fitting the fingers into rings suspended from springs, thereby forcing the fingers to push down with great strength. Bars, running parallel to the keyboard, prevented the wrists from being lifted up and down. Silent keyboards that could be adjusted to require more pressure from the fingers were advertised and sanctioned by well-known pianists. Even great artists succumbed to the allure of these machines: Kalkbrenner became a teacher in Logier's *Academie*, which promoted the use of one such device, known as the "Chiroplast," while Schumann designed his own contraption, which apparently ruined his career as a pianist by damaging the muscles of his fourth finger.

In spite of the appeal of brilliant technique, Henri Blanchard, a composer and critic, wrote in 1843, "The professor of piano ought to be an acclaimed, sought-after composer and performer…"[12] Arthur Loesser, in his book, *Men, Women and Pianos*, describes several instances where Liszt was forced to alter his programming at the last moment in order to appease an audience demanding his improvisation. Once, when Liszt included one of his Etudes in his program, an audience member exclaimed that he had not come to the concert to hear the performer practice. Liszt scheduled the Beethoven "Kreutzer" Sonata for violin and piano at another concert, at which the bored audience shouted en masse in the middle of the performance for him to stop and play his own variations on an opera theme. Liszt was forced to satisfy the audience, after which the violinist returned to finish the sonata.

The task of training pianists in the art of composition and improvisation fell upon piano teachers, and later, conservatories, which offered special courses in music theory and form and analysis. Czerny, well known as a piano pedagogue, also wrote a method book, *The School of Composition*, as well as a book on improvisation, in which he instructs how to write and improvise sonatas, minuets, rondos and other popular forms of the day.

Even two hundred years later, the lure of impressing an audience with piano technique is still the driving force for many pianists. Nevertheless, the trivial compositions of the nineteenth century have disappeared into the back of the historian's closet, while the music of Beethoven, Schumann, Schubert, and Chopin has emerged as the lasting expression of that century. Compositions by these masters demand a technique that is not an end in itself, but rather, serves the profound music that they created. Consequently, it is vital that present-day musicians be trained in understanding the compositions they play, as well as in the technical demands of effective performance. It is in this vein that Jaques-Dalcroze, at the turn of the twentieth century, sought to instill in his students the capacity to transcend the mere physical approach to music and develop into artists.

---

[12] Arthur Loesser, *Men, Women and Pianos*. (New York: Simon and Schuster, 1954), 383.

Teaching Rhythm

Rhythm defies a verbal description; it must be experienced. Moreover, merely listening to a rhythm does not ensure understanding. Active participation in singing and moving to rhythm is essential to grasp this fundamental concept. The Dalcrozian approach maintains that exercises away from the instrument are needed for the student to gain a physical comprehension of the elements of rhythm.

Having students count out beats and subdivisions in their music is not dependable. We have all dealt with students who, when the patterns become difficult, slow down the counting, thereby distorting the rhythm. Furthermore, we have all heard music that was played like successive collections of beats, without a sense of direction or plan for the piece as a whole. What is lacking is the physical experience of internalizing the beat, meter, and phrase.

Sample Lessons

Adele, a piano major in college, had to perform Liszt's "Un Sospiro" in several days and asked if I would coach her. I agreed and listened to her performance. After playing through the opening pages, she stopped and said, "I am having trouble making sense of this piece." I had noticed that, although the notes had been learned, she had overlooked one of the issues confronting the pianist at the start of the piece. The meter is 12/8, with 16th notes in the left hand. However, the nuance in her playing sounded like a meter of 3/8.

"Come away from the piano."

"Clap four times."

"Put each in a different place."

Adele started to the left of her body and proceeded to the right of her body with four claps.

"Repeat and release the knees."

As she returned to the left to repeat the pattern, she bent her knees, then moved to the right as she rose up. The claps were performed with a *crescendo*.

"Say 'ta' with each clap."

Now the claps representing the 4-beat meter of 12/8 were connected in a *crescendo*, culminating on the first of each group of four; they were no longer discrete units, but parts of a unified measure.

"Now sing the melody to the first bar, while you continue the four claps."

As she attempted to do this, she realized that her beat had to be much larger and slower to accommodate the speed of the piece. As she sang the melody, she made a *crescendo*, leading to the first beat of the next measure.

"Go to the piano and play that first bar."

When she began again, she realized that she had been singing the melody at a much quicker tempo and that the continuous 16ths in the left hand were difficult to match with the melody.

"Sing the melody while you play the left-hand part."

Now the left-hand part was molded within the 4 beats and marked by a crescendo that supported the crescendo in the melody. She was quite pleased with the results, and left the piano in order to move and sing more of the melody. As she sang again, she noticed for the first time that the melodic phrase extended well beyond the first few measures and proceeded to a climax point. When she returned to the piano to play, the piece had begun to come alive, with the sense of the Subsidiary Gesture of meter, within the Fundamental Gesture of a long, sustained movement, leading to her point of climax. She now had found a voice in the music.

Frank, a blind student I have worked with, possessed a remarkable ear for music. He had asked me to coach him in an extracurricular course, dealing with improvising in the style of various 20th century composers. His first assignment was to listen to several pieces by Debussy and try to synthesize some of the style characteristics. He had been listening to *Pour le Piano* and thought he might try to improvise a sarabande in the Debussy style.

As he began to play, it was clear that he had captured the harmonic and melodic idiom wonderfully. However, although the phrases had a degree of clarity, a Fundamental Gesture was not evident, and the playing was dull.

"Have you ever moved to the rhythm of a sarabande?"

After his negative reply, I asked him to come away from the piano so that we might move to the rhythm of the music. Typically, the sarabande, in 3-beat meter, contains the rhythm of quarter/half. Because the half note occurs on the second beat, the meter is disrupted. Because it is important to sense that quality of movement, we stepped forward on the first quarter and then "dipped" on the half note for its full length, bending the knees slowly. We held hands while we moved, so that he could feel my weight being lowered, and he matched my movements. After several trials, we linked the quarter/half note bars into a phrase: q/h, q/h, qqq, qqq. At the end of the phrase, we turned around and headed in the opposite direction. We practiced the phrase several times, and I then asked him to improvise a melody with his voice, as we stepped the pattern again.

"Return to the piano and play your improvisation."

Now, in addition to the wonderful sense of pitch understanding that his playing demonstrated, his whole body was visibly activated as he played. These were not distracting movements; rather, they were necessary whole-body movements that were setting the phrase in motion. He had found a Fundamental Gesture in our dance that was guiding him to connect the details of the melody and harmony into a unified, meaningful piece.

Discussion:

In both lessons described above, we had the same goal of finding a Fundamental Gesture from which we could connect the details. However, our approaches were slightly different. In the case of the Liszt piece, we started with the Subsidiary Gesture of meter. Once that underlying sense was achieved, Adele could expand that sense of meter–the first level of phrasing–to the whole passage. In the second example, Frank needed a sense of the dance as a whole, in order to find a Fundamental Gesture. He also needed a physical sense of the Subordinate beats—especially, the release of weight on the second beat–in order to establish the sense of *élan* appropriate to the dance.

In our examples, there was no need to have the students "count" the beats. Once the feeling for the beat/meter/phrase had been physically inculcated, the student had internalized the timing, space and dynamics of those parameters. The beat was certainly present in the performance, but there was a flexibility in the quality of the beats, motion forward and then holding back slightly.

> *From its birth, music has registered the rhythms of the human body, of which it is the complete and idealized sound image.*[13]

Teaching Technique

Joan Last writes in her text, *The Young Pianist*, "…it is the arm that steers the hand to the required position, so that the fingers can play their part without any sense of strain."[14] Last gives an example of a beginning exercise to be done at the first lesson, which is designed to impress upon the student that the genesis of movement at the piano originates with the larger muscles. She calls it "Run and Jump." The action is to "run" through the trichord (C-D-E), then "jump" to a different octave and repeat the pattern.

The freedom of this keyboard game can be generalized to movement of the whole body. For instance, the following lessons are a telling demonstration.

---

[13] Emile Jaques-Dalcroze, *Rhythm, Music and Education,* ed. Cynthia Cox, trans. Frederick Rockwell, (New York: A.S. Barnes and Co., 1935), 3–4.
[14] Joan Last, *The Young Pianist,* ed. (London: Oxford University Press, 1972), 21–22.

Sample Lessons

Mandy, an advanced student, was having technical problems with the Gigue in Bach's French Suite V. She told me that she was unsure of how fast the piece should be played. After hearing her play for a few measures, it became clear that her idea of speed was to play the triplet eighths as fast as she could. By focusing solely on the Supraficial gestures, she played in a hurried and unsteady fashion. Her performance did not have the sense of lilt appropriate for the dance.

"Follow me."

Standing next to her, I demonstrated short hops, alternating twice on one leg and then twice on the other. On the second hop of each leg, I swung the opposing leg slightly in front of the one hopping. I repeated the hops for the other leg. Once Mandy had mastered the steps, I went to the piano and improvised music in 6/8 meter that put three eighths on each hop. (Handel's Gigue from Suite in Gm, G.124, is representative.)

"Come to the piano and see if you can imitate the hops with your hand on the fallboard."

Mandy dropped her arm, supported by her second and third fingers, onto the fallboard. There was a springing action in the whole arm that imitated the hops in the feet. The arm seemed light and free.

"Now try that on the keys."

She was able to maintain the same freedom.

"Add two ascending scale steps."

She dropped onto middle C with her second finger and then, as she lifted her arm, she played the consecutive notes D and E. (The desired technique is to use one basic motion, the drop and roll, to play all three notes.) At first, she reverted to playing the notes, using three separate finger motions; to remedy this, we reestablished the "hop" by playing with the second finger alone.

"Follow me."

I played three sets of ascending trichords and ended on middle C: CDE, DEF, BCD, C. I asked her to repeat various patterns in canon, following me.

"Now you make up your own patterns."

Mandy improvised several ascending patterns and tried descending thirds. She never lost the basic technique of the drop and roll.

"Return to your piece."

When Mandy started to play, she immediately maintained the sense of the hops in the right-hand triplets. However, she soon retreated to her old habits after several measures. In order to renew her physical memory, I hopped near the piano, so that, by watching me, she once again established the Subordinate beat-grouping of three notes. She remarked that the lesson had helped her find a "right tempo," and she now had a physical sensation of the movements that guided her to maintain the tempo.

Charlie was having some technical problems with the Schubert Impromptu, Op. 90, No. 2, that had led to pain in his right arm. I knew that activating the larger muscles with an improvisation exercise would revise his movements and lead to more efficient use of the body.

"Imitate the movement I make."

Standing and facing the student, with my left hand extended above my head to the left of my body, I bent my knees and swept my arm down toward the floor and back up in the shape of a figure eight. The downward movement generated the momentum to rise back up to the starting position. Charlie mirrored the movement several times.

"Make sounds to match the movement."

Charlie improvised vocal syllables, starting with "ee," high in his voice, when his arm was at the top, and modifying the sound to "oo," low in his voice, when his arm was at its lowest point.

"Improvise music on the piano that fits the movement."

He went to the piano and, after a few attempts, settled on a *glissando* that traveled down the keyboard and back again. However, there was too large a pause at the change of direction. Charlie picked up a tennis ball in one hand and made the same *glissando*. Now, a smile appeared as he was able to capture the essence of the movement. There was even a *decrescendo* as the arm glided to the left on the keyboard and a *crescendo* as it ascended. That seemed to capture the nuance of the change from "ee" to "oo."

"Move away from the piano and imitate me again in movement and vocal sound."

Now I began with the same movement, but upon repeating it, made variations: 1. quicker in speed, 2. shorter in distance, 3. more energetic, 4. less so. Charlie paid close attention, trying to follow me.

"Now you lead."

Charlie did his best to throw me off with unexpected changes and ended the game with a dramatic gesture upward.

"Play an improvisation at the piano, based on that exercise."

Charlie used balls in both hands and produced a remarkable piece that expressed, in sound, the movements he had just created. It had a clear shape: a beginning, marked by an opening *glissando* as a motif; shorter, more dramatic *glissandos* in the middle, punctuated by rapid *martellato* alternating clusters; and ending with a rising *glissando*, marked by a *crescendo*.

"Well done. Now let's hear the piece you have been practicing."

Charlie began to play the Schubert Impromptu. After several bars, he faltered.

"Play the right-hand part, using the ball in your hand."

This was awkward, especially in mm. 3 and 4, where the melody moves by half steps. However, he gradually became more comfortable with the technique, so that he was even able to incorporate the left hand. Returning to the actual notes, playing with both hands, he realized that some of his technical problems were a result of not activating the larger muscles of the upper arm and back, as well as not shifting the weight in the feet to help with the finger action.

As Charlie finished this portion of the lesson, he thought it would be fun to choreograph more of the right-hand passage for tennis ball and left hand. He could see the benefit of sensing the overarching Fundamental Gesture, the shift of weight from one place to another, and the Associative Gesture of the figure eight, as aids to the fleetness of the Superficial Gestures at the fingertips.

Discussion:

Concerning piano technique, Russell Sherman writes, "For the legs initiate the stroke; the legs begin and close the cycle of physical coordination; the grounding of the feet reinforces the sensation of stability and its counterpart, soaring."[15] In contrast, numerous pedagogy texts open with an exercise that calls for the student to repeatedly play middle C with the thumb of the right hand, followed by D with the forefinger. It *seems* like such an obvious place to start. After all, we play the piano with fingers, and middle C is the genesis of much study in music. Yet, having begun this way as a young student, I noticed as I gained experience that we actually play the piano with our whole body. My focus had been on the proper finger and hand position, and I was at first incredulous when people suggested paying attention to the upper arm, shoulder, torso, legs and feet. After all, when I attended a concert, everyone wanted to sit so they could see the acrobatic hands, not watch the position of the legs. Eventually, it was in Eurhythmics classes that I realized I could play an instrument better when I involved the whole body.

As a way to prepare students to integrate their movements for musical expression, ask the student to stand and imagine four dots on the body: one at the top of the sternum, one on the navel and one on the underside of

---

[15] Russell Sherman *Piano Pieces* (New York: North Point Press), 1997, 18.

each of the wrists. Imagine that the dot on the chest is being gently lifted, then the navel lifted, and then the wrists. Take a walk and experience this sensation throughout the body as the teacher improvises appropriate music (e.g., Beethoven's Sonata, Op. 14, No. 2). The student may now go to the piano and try to maintain these feelings of good posture while seated.

At the bench, the feet must be in contact with the floor or, for smaller students, a footstool. As Russell Sherman states above, playing the piano involves the whole body, and this starts with the feet. Try lifting your feet off the floor as you sit at the bench and you quickly realize the disadvantage faced by students whose feet do not reach the floor. When contact is made, an immediate release of tension is experienced throughout the body. The result, in terms of playing, is freer motions.

Beyond the positioning of the body, the inspiration for musical technique is fueled by the imagination. Russell Sherman writes:

> *The idea of technique is consistently misunderstood. People think that piano technique is a matter of double thirds, fast octaves, and such specialized tricks, analogous to the current debasement of figure skating into nothing more than a series of triple axels and toe loops separated by long intervals of coasting and prayer. Technique, like poetry, is but handmaiden to the music, and should be entirely at the service of the imagination. Without imagination there is no technique, only facility.*[16]

In Charlie's lesson, our intent was to awaken the technical skills to play the Schubert Impromptu, using improvisation as the catalyst. We stimulated the larger muscles that serve as support for the hands and fingers. Charlie became more and more concerned with the musical effect and less with the physical necessities of the *glissando*. At that juncture, the technique served the imagination. The approach through imagination, rather than the "correct" position, is sensible when we notice that bodies are so different physically. How can one hand position possibly be right for every person?

In a famous documentary film of Vladimir Horowitz at 90, the virtuoso is seen sitting in a room offstage, while a videotape is replaying

---

[16] Russell Sherman, *Piano Pieces* (New York: North Point Press, 1997), 6.

what he had just performed. A young student enters the room and summons up the courage to ask the famous pianist why he plays with flat fingers. Horowitz responds, "I do not play with flat fingers," whereupon, the student points to the video and says, "But, Mr. Horowitz, you do." Horowitz looks up at the video and then turns to the student and says matter-of-factly, "I play with flat fingers."

Our goal, in terms of technique, is to help the student develop, through exercises, a general sense of the body in its optimum posture for movement. Then, we seek to find exercises that stimulate the student's creative impulse to make music. Our vehicle is that of engaging the whole body in movement and translating those movements into sound through improvisation. Although we may make suggestions about technique to the student, we appreciate that each body is different and that it is the student's imagination that is the link to a serviceable technical mastery.

Teaching Music Reading

Vision therapists, who deal with problems of dyslexia, claim that music reading is one of the most complex activities that depend on the sense of sight. Indeed, experts report that latent dyslexia can become apparent after people begin studying an instrument. Those suffering with this impairment are able to read words, albeit slowly, because they can fixate on a word without losing the train of thought. However, reading music does not permit this lingering on difficult spots, because music requires maintaining a constant flow. The problems are intensified in the case of pianists, who must grasp two or more lines of music at once. Dyslexia should be suspected in bright and talented students who read far below their playing level.

All pianists have to work at reading; it is an absolute necessity if one wants a career as a musician. There are numerous elements that are factors in the development of good reading skills. Pianists should be trained to keep their eyes on the music while reading. Another element that is often neglected is developing the student's internal sense of beat and meter. Reading music at the piano requires that there be a constant flow. When we interrupt the flow in the course of reading—to go back and correct a note, for instance—we are not reading, but practicing to learn the piece. A good sight-reader never stops the music's forward movement.

Eurhythmics in the studio can be a powerful tool in addressing problems of reading. A strong internal sense of beat and meter must be established to give students a foundation for good reading, enabling them to go beyond playing "collections of beats." (Our book, *The Rhythm Inside*, offers a number of examples on a compact disc to aid this accomplishment.)

Earlier, in Chapter Two on Props, we list the trampoline as a useful rhythmic instrument. The regularity of bounces sets a steady beat that is much more exciting than a metronome. Here is a possible scenario for using the trampoline to establish a strong sensation of beat and meter. When the student is centered on the trampoline, ready to go, the teacher says:

"Keep your bounces steady. Count '1, 2, 3.'"

"Sing '1, 2, 3' on triad notes."

"Clap on each count. Be sure to move your arms in a circle for each beat."

"Here is a hand drum. Tap on '1.'"

"Tap on '2, 3.'"

The teacher can select a rhythm from the piece to be sight-read and feed the components to the student as he bounces.

After a suitable time bouncing (watch students' stability and don't tire them), come back to the floor and continue the beat by bouncing the knees lightly, with a deeper bend on "1." Move the beat to the arms, then to the music rack. Next, sit down at the piano and, without breaking the metrical continuity, begin reading the rhythm of the piece.

"What is the meter?" the teacher asks. After receiving a correct answer, the teacher says, "Show the meter by tapping along the edge of the reading desk." The student puts her right hand in place toward the left of the reading desk and with each beat, moves toward the right. "1, 2, 3, 4." Her arm then rises and quickly returns to the left location of "1." This long movement, requiring more energy, carries the flow from "4" to "1," physically emphasizing the uplift of the anacrusis and the landing on the crusis. Students who make a habit of using this technique during practice at home develop the capacity to listen inside for the sensation of tempo and continuity of meter and beats. With this kind of preparation, they can plan their entrance and be ready to "go with the flow."

The beat and meter movement can be done with the left arm as well, of course.

"Show the meter with your left arm."

"Now tap with your right hand only on beat 1."

"Switch hands."

"Tap two eighths on beat 3."

These quick changes keep the student thinking and help develop control and versatility. Throughout this game, the feeling of the beat and the meter are being strengthened for carrying the music of the composition the student is about to sight-read or perform.

Sample Lesson

Kent, a 12-year-old piano student who had a fine natural ear, had great difficulty with note-reading. He persisted in stopping and trying to correct his mistakes. I devised a plan, based on Dalcroze principles, for discouraging that habit.

"Let's count the balls."

I had placed four balls, equally spaced on the piano rack, to represent a bar of four beats. On a sheet of enlarged staff paper behind the balls, I had placed numbers, written in different sizes (1-2-3-4), over each ball. Kent said the numbers dynamically, according to the size of the number. Further, after saying "1" loudly, he spoke 2, 3, and 4 with a *crescendo*.

"**Point to the numbers as you say them.**"

Now he not only incorporated a *crescendo*, but he enlarged his movements as he spoke more loudly.

"**Keep repeating.**"

Each time he got to beat 4, he would return to beat 1 with a *crescendo*. Then I took away the ball under beat 2. He still pointed to the place where the second ball had been; however, his voice was silent. Gradually, I took away all the balls, while he continued to point silently. The *crescendo* was still evident in his movements, and even his breathing was coordinated, so that he exhaled strongly on beat 1.

"**Now, no movement.**"

Kent continued to feel the beat internally, but fought hard not to move. I could still see little twitches, as he tried to retain the beat without movement. Again I said, "**No movement.**"

"**When I say 'Speak,' you say the appropriate number on the next beat.**"

At first, he had trouble retaining the beat over a period of time. With practice, he became quite adept at the game and over the next few lessons, we changed the meters. He had been trained to sense where he was in the measure, no matter what the distraction.

We proceeded to some actual music scores and we played similar games.

"**Here's the tempo; you play only the first note of each measure.**"

"**Play only the second beat.**"

"**When I say 'Stop,' stop playing but keep reading.**"

"**If I say 'Play,' start to play.**"

Gradually, Kent trained himself to keep going. He was learning to connect his visual field to the internal clock of meter that had been strongly ingrained from the earlier exercises.

The internal memory of beat and meter was established in the activities just described, through the strong sensation of large-muscle movement performing the taps and the anacrusis-crusis return. Students can also use large muscles in moving through physical space to help develop their "map" of pitch locations. Beside my piano, within easy reach of the keyboard, hangs a grand staff, made of 10 wooden dowels, five for each staff, with a short rod for middle C hanging in between. This is a favorite item to play with when students are learning their note locations.

John was ready to begin note reading. I took the wooden staff[17] off the wall and moved away from the piano.

"Come stand opposite me."

I held the staff between us, so that either of us could grasp a dowel (line) or extend a hand between two dowels (space).

"Here is a ladder. Grasp the bottom rung and say, 'Line.'"

"Now put your hand between the first and second ones and say, 'Space.'"

John timidly touched the dowel with a fingertip and pointed at the space.

"Let's make that stronger. Put your hand around the rung tightly, as if you were hanging from a trapeze."

John looked at me with an air of challenge and grabbed the dowel with all his might.

"Good! Now open your hand quite flat and push it between the rungs. Say, 'Space'."

John caught the idea and traveled up the whole staff, saying "Line" and "Space" at a steady pace, maintaining a sense of continuity, which

---

[17] See Chapter 2, p. 32 for a picture of the wooden staff.

is the basis of good sight-reading. We reinforced the words and movements with light knee bounces.

Soon, John was ready to place several notes on the staff. I renewed the knee bounces and grasped the bottom line of the treble staff.

"**Here is E; here is F**" (hand between first and second dowels); "**here is G**" (hand grasping the second dowel). I spoke these words rhythmically.

"**Say it back to me.**"

John matched the tempo and copied my performance. Then we began variations: I revised the order, I said the name so that John could show the note location, or I showed the location and John said the name. We came back to this exercise at every lesson, gradually adding notes until both staves were secure.

Joseph was consistently missing the top note of an interval starting on G (second line, treble). Instead of F (top line, treble), he was playing D (fourth line, treble).

"**Show me that note on the wooden staff.**"

In order to do this, he had to focus on the exact location in the printed music. He turned to the staff hanging on the wall within reach and grasped the top line.

"**Name the note.**"

He remembered from naming games that the highest line was F, and realized immediately that he had not looked carefully enough at the location on the page. Joseph said, "I knew it was higher than G and just reached for a higher note. Now I will notice and I will remember."

And indeed, his F was reliable from then on. The physical sensation of reaching up to that line and the strong grasp reinforced a sense of location and strengthened his memory.

One day, Mitzi was stumbling over a bar of music. She felt something was wrong by the end of the bar, but couldn't locate the difficulty. She tried changing the rhythm.

"No, look again."

She added a sharp to one of the notes.

"Not yet, look again."

Mitzi suddenly, of her own volition, turned to the wooden staff and located the notes, one by one. She said delightedly, "Oh, there it is! There are TWO A's, not just one."

Mitzi discovered that she had been missing a repeated note in the passage and had simply needed to look more carefully at the line/space pattern. Moving her arm and hand at the wooden staff gave her a larger physical experience of the melody than she was getting through her eyes and fingers.

This experience of having a student turn to the wooden staff for assistance in identifying the printed notes has happened numerous times, even with students who have studied for several years. Justin, when looking through a piece, still occasionally assures himself of his low bass notes by checking their location on the wooden staff.

Jenny stood near the piano while I played some seconds.

"Listen to these sounds. They are called seconds. Seconds are neighboring notes. Here is how you can recognize them in your music."

I stood facing her while holding the wooden staff between us.

"Grab any line. Put your other hand in the space above. That is what a second looks like."

"Put your hand in any space. Now use your other hand to grab the next line."

Jenny wondered whether she should go up or down.

"Either way. A second is always a line note and a space note next to each other."

"Show some more seconds. Higher. Lower."

"Now go to the piano, and using only white keys, play seconds."

"Which is the line note?" (or space note)

Later, we used the same procedure with thirds. First, I played thirds to set the sound in the student's ear.

"Grab any line. Grab the next line up with your other hand. That interval is a third."

"Put your hand in a space. Now put your other hand in the next space, above or below."

"That interval is also a third. Thirds are made of two line notes or two space notes."

"Show some line thirds. Some space thirds. Now play some on the white keys."

"Sing one note and then the other."

Subsequently, Jenny found it easy to identify seconds and thirds in her written music. She also associated the sounds with the sense of space between her hands on the wooden staff, as well as on the keyboard.

This kind of exercise is extended in later lessons to other intervals. It emphasizes the look of the interval (line/space) by requiring the student to place a whole hand in the correct location. (Students have become so fascinated with the process that they have even volunteered to play their melodies on the wooden staff, singing along!) The combination of line and space for even-numbered intervals and the line/line and space/space appearance for odd-numbered intervals becomes strongly apparent in using the wooden staff. It is actually harder to see than the distances on the page and therefore, demands more conscious attention. Focusing the attention on such strategies as the line/space interval appearance on the wooden staff carries over to a more conscious awareness of what is on the page.

Along with learning the feel of interval space, we name the interval notes.

"Put a hand in bass clef second space. Name the note." ("C.")

"Put your other hand a fifth higher." (Student goes to fourth space.)

"Name the note." ("G.")

A variation starts with the note name.

"Show me B in the treble clef." (Student grabs the middle bar.)

"With your other hand, find D in the treble clef." (Student puts hand below the first line, above the short middle bar C.)

"Name the interval." ("Sixth")

More exercise comes with naming all the notes a third apart (all lines or all spaces), keeping a steady beat, which can increase in speed as skill develops. Seventh chords can be built, and series of fourths. Any such game played on the wooden staff strengthens the students' sense of place and space, letter name and interval, by removing them from the small movements of the fingers and letting their minds concentrate on larger sensations of distance and of rise and fall. These memories then are available to guide the fingers in their movements at the keyboard.

Discussion:

William Richards, in his article, "Music Reading at the Piano," writes:

> *Music reading is NOT music spelling. Music spelling is individual note naming; music reading involves interval recognition, and to be effective must establish relationships among notes. Note naming (music spelling) possesses little value unless linked with interval recognition.*[18]

---

[18] William Richards, "Music Reading at the Piano," in Yvonne Enoch and James Lyke, *Creative Piano Teaching*, (Champaign: Stipes Publishing Co., 1997), 42.

The narratives from our studios support the notion that music reading involves "establishing relationships among notes." The Dalcroze approach intensifies this relationship among notes by transforming the visual into physical sensation. The wooden staff increases the awareness of musical space; the ball exercises induce the feeling of continuity. There is power in the physical solidity of the staff, and the act of pointing to the balls demands big-muscle movements, which stimulate students' memory.

Our interest is to provide exercises that might spur the teacher to find creative ways to approach a score, making it musical from the first moment of exposure. With a review of Chapter 2 (the list of props), innumerable games can be invented to change note reading into music reading. This approach works as effectively—and is as important—during a beginner's lesson on an eight-bar piece with a range of three notes as it is with a Beethoven sonata. Converting the abstract symbols of a piece of music into musical communication is what we always strive for at every level, every age, every style.

As musicians, we understand that reading the score, at best, gives us only a hazy glimpse of the composer's desires. It is the creative imagination of the musician that imbues the score, even at first glimpse, with possibilities. Letting ourselves move physically with the notes of the music helps us realize the music that is between the notes.

Teaching Ear Training

Julie, a 10-year-old beginning piano student, was arriving for her fifth lesson. She was used to working away from the keyboard. At this lesson, I wanted to introduce some exercises to increase her listening skills.

"Show me a hop."

As I sat at the keyboard, Julie made a hop with both feet. I translated the hop into music on the piano, with a tennis ball in my hand, to coincide with her tempo.

"Put that hop in your arms…in your hands."

Keeping the same tempo, she bounced both arms up and then let them fall back. Then she bounced with her fingers, while the rest of her body was still activated, a willing support for the acrobatic hands.

"Take the ball and improvise some hops."

At first, the playing was stiff. Then, she realized that merely pushing down the notes did not give quite the desired effect. Instead, by playing quick, short, ascending *glissandos*, the effect of the hop was achieved. Julie noticed that her whole arm was in play.

"Show me how you go 'blading' (skating)."

At first, she looked reluctant, but after several tries, she imitated the gliding moves associated with roller blades by alternating the sliding of each foot forward. I accompanied with an improvisation.

"Put the glide in your arms...in your hands."

Again, Julie came to the piano, with tennis ball in hand, and tried to realize the "blading" motion in sound. Her first attempts were thwarted because, although she captured the slower tempo and softer dynamics with a more sustained legato *glissando*, the abrupt halt between the *glissandos* did not capture the sustained activity. Julie discovered that the pedal helped her maintain the sense of continuity in the motion.

Now, I presented her with a 2-measure pattern in 4/4 meter: two half notes in the first measure and three quarter notes and a quarter rest in the second. We decided that the blade motion was called for by the half notes and the hops could be represented by the quarter notes. Julie used the tennis ball to improvise a short piece based on the pattern. Later, she used both hands without the ball to make up a new piece.

Janice, a cello student in my theory class, was having trouble memorizing Saint-Saens' "The Swan" for her applied lesson. I asked her whether she had tried to sing the melody. She replied that no one had ever asked her to do that before.

"As you sing the melody, follow the shape of the line with your arm."

As she sang, she followed the shape of the melody, but her movements were rigid.

"Start again, but as you sing, shift the weight from your left foot to your right for the first phrase."

Now the movement was much more flowing, but she became aware that she did not know where the phrase ended. After another attempt, she decided that the phrase ended at the high B at the start of the fourth measure.

"Sing again and show me, in space, where the highest note is."

She positioned a note slightly above her head and said, "It's the last note of the phrase."

"Relate that to the first pitch of the piece."

She sang the first note, G, and placed it slightly lower than the B.

"Now sing from the starting pitch up to the highest note."

When she sang, she filled in the interval of a third with the intervening scale step and noticed that the highest note of the phrase was the third degree of the scale.

"Sing again and show me the lowest note."

She sang through the piece until she found the low E, which she placed slightly below her knee.

"Sing the melody again, but fit the whole melody between your lowest and highest pitches."

It took several times before she became comfortable with the process; however, the spacing and flow of the melody were apparent, and the individual scale degrees were more obvious. Now the arm indicated qualities of movement in three-dimensional space. When she sang the E in the first measure, it seemed to float and hesitate before proceeding downward. When she finished, she exclaimed, "That low note is an E. I noticed I proceeded up by scale steps to the G."

"Sing once more, with more sensitivity to the leaps in the melody."

Now, her arm and hand moved more carefully through the melody, so that the spacing and quality of the notes were more evident. Later, when she played the passage on the cello, there was meaning in each note. No longer were they individual places on the finger board; they were linked in a melody with a sense of direction. She was hearing the music on a deeper level.

Discussion:

Our goal in this section is to show that ear training based on Dalcroze principles involves movement of the whole body to music. When we react to the sounds in this manner, we are attending to and concentrating on the connection between our movement and sound. Far from making ear training a separate issue in the lesson, we show how it can be incorporated into hearing all the subtleties in a piece at hand: direction of the melody; variation in intensity, rubato, and articulation; as well as intervals, key shifts, and so forth. The ear and body together must hear all of these things. With this approach, ear training in the lesson will be much more than naming note values, intervals and pitches.

A key to developing this skill lies in singing. Great musicians of all ages have insisted that the secret to playing an instrument was to sing through the instrument. From the outset, students should sing passages in their pieces. In the lesson with Janice, one avenue to developing her inner hearing of "The Swan"—and thus memorizing her piece—was to sing through the melody, with the support of physical gesture. While discerning individual pitches and intervals, she also heard them in the context of a Fundamental Gesture. The Supraficial Gestures were carefully nuanced, while "tucked in" to the larger shape.

Ear training in the Dalcroze tradition is a misnomer; "body training" more accurately expresses the connection between the sounds we hear and how we interpret them. The feeling for time, space and energy of music begins with the physical perception of the sounds we hear.

Practicing and Memorization

Eliza, seven years old, was playing Johann Sebastian Bach's "Minuet in G" from the Anna Magdalena Notebook. Her teacher had told me that she had performed this piece at a very high level some months ago; however, this particular performance was full of wrong notes and lacked any sense of continuity. Further, her performance of the two quarter-note G's in the second measure transmitted a sense that she did not have the feeling for the quality of the beat in this dance in 3-beat meter. I had the sense that in the past she had played it from memory (confirmed later by her teacher), but now she was trying to read it from the score. Her problem was one of how to practice after a hiatus and how to strengthen her memory.

"Come dance with me," I said, when she had finished.

"Follow me."

We placed our right-hand palms together and proceeded in clockwise fashion in a small circle, taking a step for each beat. On the second beat of bar 2, we did not transfer the weight to the foot, but merely touched the ground with a toe point, in order to reflect the quality of that beat. On the third beat of that bar, we changed direction and joined our left palms to proceed counterclockwise. We repeated the steps for bars 3 and 4; however, in bars 5 to 8, we kept walking, in a clockwise path, until we reached the eighth bar, where we faced each other and bowed.

"Please play the piece again."

This time there was a decided sense of continuity, and there were no note stumbles. She sounded like a different performer. We had reawakened the Fundamental Gesture in her playing. Still, the nuances of the second and fourth bars (the toe points) were not evident in the playing.

"Let's go back to our dance."

This time I asked Eliza to sing as we danced, and we practiced the toe points with singing, until her singing reflected the motion of the toe points.

"Let's play the first four measures again."

Now, when she arrived at the repeated quarters, they were not all played in the same way; rather, the second beat was softer and lighter, while the third beat had a sense of lift, representing our turn at that point in the dance.

"Now let's rehearse our bow."

I had noticed in the recent performance that the eighth bar, with the *appoggiatura* B-A, did not reflect the repose felt in the bow. After several rehearsals of singing, Elizabeth played the first eight bars again, and the audience was clearly amazed at the transformation. It was now a polished performance; there was a sense that the Fundamental Gesture was completed by a slight sense of repose in the eighth bar, and she had not lost the beautiful shaping of the Subsidiary inner beats.

> *Some way must be found to practice for performance at the outset, not after habits unrelated to performance have been established. Not stopping a rhythmic procedure to the end is a demand for an exciting performance. It must be practiced first, for first habits can persist.*[19]

The Dalcroze emphasis on sensing music through movement goes directly to performance. Making a "first habit" of beginning the study of a composition by moving and singing sets the student in a position to form other good playing habits. With the messages from the body, the ear attends to the connections between notes, the arms feel the weight of beginning and release, the body moves subtly as the music develops, and player and listener rejoice in "an exciting performance."

---

[19] Abby Whiteside, *Indispensables of Piano Playing and Mastering the Chopin Etudes and Other Essays*. (Portland: Amadeus Press, 1997), 145.

Works Cited

Agay, Denes, ed. *Teaching Piano.* New York: Yorktown Music Press, 1981.

Enoch, Yvonne, and James Lyke, ed. *Creative Piano Teaching.* Champaign: Stipes Publishing Co., 1997.

Last, Joan. *The Young Pianist*, 2d ed. London: Oxford University Press, 1972.

Loesser, Arthur. *Men, Women and Pianos.* New York: Simon and Schuster, 1954.

Schnebly-Black, Julia, and Stephen Moore. *The Rhythm Inside: Connecting Body, Mind and Spirit.* Van Nuys: Alfred Publishing, Inc., 2003.

Sherman, Russell. *Piano Pieces.* New York: North Point Press, 1997.

CHAPTER FIVE

EXPLORATION OF COMPOSITIONS

Johann Sebastian Bach
Invention No. 8 in FM

Observations:

Johann Sebastian Bach wrote the 15 Inventions as teaching pieces for his son, Wilhelm Friedemann Bach. They were intended as guides to composition, as well as performance on the keyboard. On the title page of the 1723 autograph edition of the *Inventions and Sinfonias* (often called Two- and Three-Part Inventions), Johann Sebastian writes:

> *Sincere instruction in which lovers of keyboard music,*
> *and especially those desiring to learn to play, are*
> *shown a clear way not only (1) to learn to play*
> *cleanly in two parts, but also after further progress (2)*
> *to proceed correctly and well with three obbligato parts,*
> *and at the same time not only to compose good*
> *inventions, but to develop them well; but most of all to*
> *achieve a cantabile style in playing, and to acquire a*
> *taste for the elements of composition.*

The Two-Part Inventions, as a whole, follow similar form designs. All are pieces where two voices have equal roles. Each Invention divides roughly in half, similar to what one might expect in a binary dance movement, with a modulation to the dominant, if the piece is in major, and to the relative major, if it begins in minor. At this midpoint, Bach modulates to diatonically related keys before returning to a dominant preparation for the final cadence. Often, the closing material is a transposition of the opening material–the characteristic of rounded binary form. It is advisable for the student to incorporate the larger dimensions of the piece by internally singing the RH or LH melodic line through the whole piece and allowing the whole body to react as if it were developing choreography. Dalcroze referred to this type of study as *rythmique plastique* (moving sculpture, modeled rhythm), a way for the performer to embody the music to be performed.

Objectives:

We have selected four aspects of Invention No. 8 to discuss: (1) the Fundamental Gesture (mm. 1-2), (2) the extended eighth-note anacrusis that initiates the piece, (3) the 16th note figures that continue throughout the piece, and (4) the counterpoint in contrary motion.

(1) We begin with an exercise to help us embody the Fundamental Gesture, that encompasses the patterns of mm. 1-2 in the RH. The Fundamental Gesture involves a movement of the arm in a circle, so that m. 1 entails the Associative Gesture, "bottom" of a circle going counterclockwise, and m. 2 is the "top" of the continuous circle. Exercise 3.5 provides a model that we can modify to fit this piece:

Preparation:

T at piano, S facing the teacher and holding a scarf in the right hand.

"Make a counterclockwise circle in the air with the scarf."

T says "Bigger," or "Smaller," as preparation for the entrance of the music.

T plays music to match S's scarf movements.

"Follow my tempo."

T alters the tempo and dynamics to affect the movements of S's circles.

S should practice the scarf circles in different combinations: left arm, right arm; together, separately; clockwise, counterclockwise.

Following this exercise, the student should come to the piano and attempt to recreate the movements in sound:

> S sits at the piano, tennis ball cupped in hand, and modifies the arm movement of the scarf exercise to sweep (glissando) over the fallboard (keys covered). This technique helps the student remain focused on the Gesture, rather than trying immediately to "finger" the movement. (Again, both arms must try this movement.)

> Then S produces the same counterclockwise gesture in the following exercise:

> "Now fingers 1 and 5 (or 4) (1 and 2, 1 and 3, and so forth) in the right hand."

> "Now clockwise with the left hand."

> "Fingers 1 and 5 (1 and 2, 1 and 3, and so forth) in the left hand."

> "Both hands, 1 and 5 (1 and 2, 1 and 3, and so forth)."

right hand

left hand

> T lifts fallboard and S plays the pattern on the keyboard: two notations R.H., L.H., and so forth. Following these exercises, the student plays the first measure of the piece, while the teacher observes the performance.

> Can the student maintain the relaxed circles in the hand, as the

expanding intervals proceed through the measure?

Can the student mirror these movements in the LH when it enters in m. 2?

T calls out various note names and S plays octaves with RH, LH, and both hands.

(2) Now we are prepared to address the anacrusis, an Associative Gesture. Here we refer to a modification of Exercise 3.7:

Preparation:

T and S stand facing each other

"Watch me."

T counts six pulses, T and S put palms together on "6," fling them apart on the next "1."

T continues counting, T and S bring palms together on "5-6" and fling them apart on the next "1," then "4-5-6," and so on.

With each addition, T increases the pressure. T and S continue until cycle is completed ("2-3-4-5-6" and fling apart on "1").

"Your turn to lead."

S says the counts with *crescendo* and increases of pressure.

S returns to the piano and plays the opening measure, still utilizing the Associative Gesture ("bottom" of the circle), with a *crescendo* controlled by the upper arm. The gesture at the piano is the lower half of the Fundamental Gesture. Use the "top half" of the Fundamental Gesture to make an arc that will help initiate the next Gesture.

Try this exercise with both hands individually and together:

(3) The 16th note figure in m. 2 is controlled by the "top half" of the circular motion. From a seated position at the piano, return to Exercise 3.7; concentrate on the movement of fingers 5 to 1, 4 to 1, 3

to 1, and so forth-the top part of the circle—as opposed to the movement of fingers 1 to 5.

"Now use fingers 5 (or 4) and 1 (2 and 1, 3 and 1, and so forth) in the RH."

"Fingers 5 and 1 (2 and 1, 3 and 1, and so forth) in the LH."

The quicker 16th notes in m. 2 can now be enveloped in the Subordinate Gesture of the falling interval of the fourth: F down to C, D to A, B-flat to F.

Subordinate Gesture–Bottom Half

Subordinate Gesture–Top Half

It is advisable that each of these descending fourths be practiced individually before they are linked together. Increase the speed until they can be played like a *glissando*. This speed is not necessary for the final performance; however, by playing the fourths very quickly, the pianist becomes aware of the larger grouping which connects the figure and leads to a more secure musical performance.

The remainder of the 16th note figures in the piece are similar to those in mm. 4-6 (in the right hand and imitated in the left hand). It is interesting to realize that the "top half" includes the falling thirds.

Each of the beat patterns of 16th notes in these measures can be understood as microcosms of the Fundamental Gesture. Thus, if we focus on the first beat of the RH in m. 4, A2 to C3 is a small "lower half "of the circle, while the oscillation from Bb-C involves a tiny circular movement of its own. This 4-note figure from beat 1 to beat 2 can be practiced in two parts, until the circle A2-C3-A2 and the smaller embedded circle of C3-Bb2-C3 are secure. This same pattern (beat 1 of m. 5) appears in the LH and should be treated technically as a mirror of the RH pattern in m. 4.

Reflections:

What is the appropriate articulation for the 16th note figures?

What is the appropriate dynamic?

(4) Finally, the pianist faces the difficulty of presenting two equal voices—a critical aspect of the music from this style period. (This technique is applicable to all styles of music.) As a way to begin the study of the two voices in contrary motion, return to Exercise 3.2:

Preparation:

S holds scarves in both hands

"Make circles in contrary motion (either clockwise or counterclockwise)."

"Bigger now. Smaller now."

"Reverse direction."

T improvises music to accompany circular beat. (T could play *glissandos* with tennis balls moving in contrary motion. Chopin Etude, Op. 25, No. 9.) T uses tempo and dynamic variations to affect the change in space for S's circles.

This variation helps the student incorporate the sense of the concurrent Gestures—the RH descending in m. 2, while the LH ascends. The goal is to make sure that both lines are expressive. In m. 2, the RH loses energy as the LH needs to increase. In only a few measures of the piece do the two hands progress in parallel motion—mm. 5-6 and mm. 27-28. Because much of the piece is in canon, it may be beneficial to practice certain measures by having both hands play the right-hand part at the distance of an octave (mm. 1-7 and mm. 26-29).

After studying these four aspects, it is advisable to return to a deeper Fundamental Gesture we had discussed at the outset. Refer again to the Fundamental Gesture we explored in Exercise 3.9; however, we will employ this movement slowly, over a much greater time span.

Invention 8 exemplifies the rounded binary form we formerly discussed. There are two main sections: A-mm. 1-12, and B-mm. 12-34. Partway through the B section, the opening material returns, transposed an interval of a fourth higher, so that the piece will end on tonic. The teacher might ensure that the student is aware of these relationships by asking questions and making suggestions, such as: "Using the movement from Exercise 3.9, sing through the piece internally, as you move very slowly through the gesture."

"Aim for the climax of your movement to come at the midpoint of the piece (m. 12). At the start of the B section, repeat the Fundamental Gesture for the second half of the piece."

"Reflect on these movements. Are there other movements more appropriate? Is there an emotion or emotions that now link your movement to the Invention?"

"Try the same exercise, without the score, using a gesture that seems appropriate for you personally. Imagine the piece, in tempo, as you again repeat the gesture."

Just as the exercises are guides, so, too, it is important for performers to discover the composer's voice, as well as their own expression. By developing their own movements, they become aware of the emotions they need to transmit and develop the confidence to "say something" unique with their performance.

Robert Schumann
The Happy Farmer
Album for the Young, Op. 68, No. 10

Observations:

The *Album for the Young* in two parts called *For Children and For Adults* was composed in 1848, during Schumann's years at Dresden, where he and his family had moved, in the hope of finding rest and quiet. The pieces in this set, like those in *Scenes from Childhood*, show a sensitivity to the imagination of children. "The Happy Farmer" displays this typical characteristic by presenting a straightforward impression of vigorous buoyancy and good spirits. This is not a heavy-footed farmer in muddy boots. This is a farmer who has looked at his fields, his barns and animals, his house and family, and realized how good life can be.

The lift of anacrusic rhythm that pervades the entire piece promotes the sense of joyful movement. This forward thrust of energy is essential to a good performance. The change of texture from single-line melody to a melody doubled in the second hand, plus the presentation of the melody in the left hand, gives a student the challenge of letting this melody ride on the rhythm, while coloring it with variety. The greatest technical difficulty lies in the neccessity at certain points to play both melody and accompaniment in one hand.

Objectives:

This piece contains several musical elements which deserve attention, because they are present in so many compositions at different levels of difficulty: the anacrusic motif, which is the principal building block; the accompanying complementary beats; the shift of these two figures between right hand and left hand; the incorporation of two voices in one hand.

This first exercise is a variation of Exercise 3.10, which focuses on the Associative Gesture of Patterns. The exercise about anacrusis in the earlier examination of Bach's Invention is also worth reviewing at this point.

Preparation:

T and S stand, holding drums and facing each other.

"Copy what I do."

T taps 4 beats, while pulling the drum upwards on a diagonal slant.

"Go."

"Repeat. Be sure your wrists pull the sound out of the drum."

"You play 2 and 3; I play 1 and 4."

T and S continue repeating pattern, until T gives S a change.

"4-1."

T plays 2 and 3.

T and S maintain eye contact and move about in a "movement conversation."

"2-4."

T plays 1 and 3.

"And stop."

Be sure to return to "2-3" and "4-1," so that S is ready to carry this sensation to the piano.

Reflections:

Did S keep the drum moving?

Did you call commands so that S had just enough time to be able to change?

Did S's wrists move with flexibility on each 2-note grouping?

Variation::

T and S side by side at piano

"Bring this gesture to the keyboard." (Recall the drum movement above.)

"Play 2-3 on the fallboard in a single gesture."

T plays the 2 notes of an ascending fourth on 4-1.

"Play any two notes a third apart, on 2 and 3."

"Change to new ones."

"Play a repeated triad on 2 and 3."

"And stop."

From m. 9 (the beginning of the B section) through m. 12, and again, from m. 13 through m. 16, the RH must play the melody on 4-1, as well as the repeated accompaniment notes on 2-3. The preparation already accomplished in the previous exercises will guide the RH in combining these two impulses. The opening interval of a rising seventh in m. 9 and m. 11 as well as the rising fourth in m. 13 and m. 15 use the sideways flexibility derived from the Fundamental Gesture, while the repeated tones rely on the sensations of pulling tones out of the drum. Alternating between these two movements ensures a flexible wrist that reduces finger tension and lets the music flow in the forward pull of the Fundamental Gesture.

"Take a scarf in each hand."

"Make a big swoop upwards. Repeat several times."

"Sing the rising seventh (C-B-flat), as you perform the movement."

"Add descending notes (A-G), as your arms come down."

"Now add two small wrist movements at the top for the after-beat chords."

"Be sure to keep the feeling of the swoop up and the flow down."

It is impossible for the repeated notes in the accompaniment to be played legato, but they should be played within an awareness of the Fundamental Gesture. The melody must remain legato, to express the smooth swing of the happy farmer's song. S must learn how to divide attention to monitor both types of muscle sensation. Refer to Exercise 3.9 for review of whole-body movement with song.

Variation: T at piano, S standing nearby.

"Sing the melody with me."

"This time, move your arms to show the melody."

"Let your arms swoop and soar!"

T plays while S moves. If necessary, T sings and moves with S.

"Add light-weight steps on 2 and 3." (in place, if necessary)

"Keep the melody smooth and always moving."

Reflections:

Did S move arms freely?

Did "melody" arms keep a smooth flow, when the stepping was added?

Learning to feel the combination of the two muscle impulses will clarify what the hand must do in bars 9-16. The mental and physical understanding of a musical movement will feed from the larger muscles to the smaller, from two hands to one.

This exercise is a modification of Exercise 3.8:

Preparation:

T and S stand facing each other

"Put your right palm against my left palm; I'll guide the melody."

T and S sing the melody, as they move their hands to the rise and fall of the melody.

"Now you guide."

"I'll guide; we'll tap 2 and 3 with the other hand."

"You show the melody with one hand, tap with the other."

"Change hands: your left and my right."

These games, which emphasize the feeling of moving through the composition, establish a desire—a goal—that helps pull together all the commands needed to accomplish a musical performance. This approach does not diminish the importance of correct notes and fingering, but places them, from the first lesson, within the musical gesture. Then the student can hear and feel where the music is going.

Frédéric Chopin
Etude, Op. 10, No. 1

Observations:

Chopin had written the first Etude as early as 1829. In a letter to a friend, he wrote, "I have composed a Study in my own manner." It ushered in a new approach to the keyboard, in which the pianist must negotiate the full range of the instrument at the extremes of tempo.

In a way, this Etude pokes some technical fun at the first Prelude from *The Well-Tempered Clavier* of Johann Sebastian Bach. Bach's Prelude begins with an arpeggio of the C major triad: C1-E1-G1-C2-E2. Chopin begins his Etude an octave lower with an almost identical arpeggio: c-g-C1-E1. The "fun" occurs when Chopin extends the triad over the span of four octaves, exploiting the full range of the piano. A passage like this would have been impossible on Bach's instruments. The range of the instruments in Bach's day was much more limited, and the instruments did not have the capacity to sustain arpeggios.

This extended figure demands the full cooperation of the whole body. The left foot needs to provide an anchor; the torso needs to be coordinated, so that the whole upper body moves as a unit on the sitting bones; and the upper arm controls the quick turns of the wrist and the rapid weight shifts at the fingers. The constant repetition of a 16th note figure presents an added challenge. This fact intensifies the need for the pianist to incorporate the smaller movements into larger muscle movements—a Fundamental Gesture—so that the tension can be relieved as much as possible.

Objectives:

There are four aspects of the Etude that are particularly amenable to exercises in Eurhythmics: (1) the Fundamental Gesture (mm. 1 and 2), (2) the Subordinate Gestures that delineate the beat, (3) the dynamic accents designated by Chopin, and (4) *crescendo* and *diminuendo* associated with the Fundamental Gesture.

(1) Carl Mikuli, a student of Chopin, wrote in the preface to his edition of Chopin's Etudes:

> *According to Chopin, evenness in scale-playing and arpeggios depends...foremostly on the perfectly smooth and constant sideways movement of the hand (not step by step), letting the elbow hang down freely and loosely at all times. This movement he exemplified by a glissando across the keys.*[20]

We have used a similar technique from Exercise 3.1, in order to establish a Fundamental Gesture for this piece:

Preparation:

T at the piano, S standing and facing T

"Make gestures for the sounds you hear."

T plays *glissandi* (white keys, as well as black) throughout the full range of the keyboard, emphasizing tempo and dynamic changes.

"And stop."

S comes to the piano and imitates T's playing; T moves arms in the air to imitate S's playing.

T limits the *glissandi* to the space of the *arpeggios* in the right hand, from c-E4.

This exercise can be modified to suit several of the patterns, until the performer has the sense of the Fundamental Gesture that involves the whole body in motion.

T should reinforce this experience with questions, such as, "Where in the body does the movement begin? Do you feel tightness anywhere when you move? What imagery do you have for this Gesture? An image can help you retain the feeling of the Gesture. If you lose it, return to the *glissandi* exercise to remind the body of this shape."

---

[20]Frederic Chopin, *Etudes,* ed. Carol Mikuli, (New York: G. Schirmer, 1943), ii.

(2) Playing the repeated 16th note pattern that overlaps beat 1 to beat 2 of m. 1 needs special attention. A slight modification of Exercise 3.4 will help to remind the student of the techniques involved here:

Preparation:

T at the piano, S holding scarf in RH.

"Make a counterclockwise circle."

"Slower; now faster."

T plays *arpeggios* to match the tempo of S's circles.

"Follow the music."

T plays *arpeggios* that change in tempi; finally, so quickly that S's circles are very abrupt gestures.

"And stop."

S can now put down the scarf and come to the piano. Without actually playing, S reproduces the quick, circular movement with the right hand in a counterclockwise direction over the keys. Using the same gesture, S plays the 16th note figures, stopping after each group of four. If S is pushing a finger down for each note, rather than linking them in a single gesture, T should remind S of the snap-like wrist movement that resulted from the quick upper-arm movements when making the quick circles with the scarf. S should focus on shifting the weight of the arm, as the fingers pass over the keys. This lessens any extraneous movement and helps S concentrate on the Subordinate Gesture (snap of the wrist), which will later be enveloped by the Fundamental Gesture.

(3) Over every beat of the first two measures of the Etude, Chopin wrote an accent mark. At first glance, one cannot imagine that Chopin intended each beat to be accented so strongly. However, as one becomes comfortable with the Fundamental Gesture and the Subordinate Gestures for the beats, it is apparent that something more is needed to help the player find relief from the constant repetitions.

The solution comes from Chopin's markings. They indicate a hierarchy, in terms of dynamics, that needs to be observed, in order for the musical and technical goals to be achieved. We turn to a modification of Exercise 3.6 for a lesson on accents:

Preparation:

T at the piano and S facing T

"Make a gentle fist."

"When you hear a loud sound, open and quickly close again."

T plays steady stream of quiet chords (***pp***) *non legato*, then interjects a louder chord.

T continues to play steady beats with chords, changing the length of time between accents and the dynamic level of the various accents (***mp*** – ***ff***).

"And stop."

Reflections:

Did S respond in a timely manner, without excess tension?

Did S vary the size of the movement according to the dynamic changes of the accents?

S returns to the piano and plays the first 16th note *arpeggio*; however, now an accent is added to the last note of the group. T can suggest that S stop on the accented note and relive the feeling of the quick reflex action, obtained in the previous exercise, by returning to the gentle fist. S should practice each of the repeated *arpeggios* in this manner, so that the accented note has the feeling of a tiny rest stop in the path of the Fundamental Gesture.

The descending pattern is slightly different, because now the accent must be on the first note of the figure. Therefore, the performer has to drop onto the first note, then let the weight quickly dissipate over the other notes of the group.

Finally, the task becomes to link up the Subsidiary Gestures of the beats and envelop them in the Fundamental Gesture. The secret is to continue the circle that we used to express the quick *arpeggio* in the earlier exercise. The performer makes a quick snap of the opening four notes (bottom half of the circle), ending with an accent, and then continues the counterclockwise circle (top half of the circle), ever so quickly, to prepare for the next snap. Of course, for the descending figure, the performer needs to reverse the two parts of the circle. The weight is released onto the first note, and the hand follows the arc of the top half of a counterclockwise circle. Then the wrist continues the lower half of the circle to prepare for the next descending figure.

(4) Dalcroze's First Rule of Nuance states that, with exceptions, ascending melodies should make a *crescendo* and descending melodies, a *decrescendo*.

"Stand, face, and put your palm against mine."

"Lean forward gradually. Feel the changes in pressure."

"Now lean back and feel the pressure lessen."

"Let's do this again and 'sing' the melody with *crescendo* up, *diminuendo* down."

"Let the feeling of leaning into the music and then backing off affect the flow of the Fundamental Gesture."

Once the piece has been studied in detail, it is important to incorporate the smaller gestures into a *plastique* for the whole Etude. This helps the student focus on a Fundamental Gesture for the background structure that will clarify climaxes over longer time periods and conserve strength by controlling the dynamic scheme. The form of this Etude follows a pattern that Chopin adopted for most of the Etudes. It begins with an opening period, "A" section, with a tonicization of V in mm. 5-8 in the opening phrase, and then an imperfect authentic cadence on I at the end of the period, in m. 15.

This is followed by modulation to the relative minor, "B section." A sequential passage leads to the return of the material from the opening, "A1," which is extended by a codetta at m. 69. The overall shape of this Etude is A (mm. 1-16) B (mm. 17-43) A1 (44-79).

Using the Gesture from Exercise 3.8, and using these main divisions as points of reference, sing through the bass line, as you move slowly through the Gesture. Find your own points of climax within the movement. When you perform the piece, let this background Gesture serve as a unifying force in your playing. Mikuli reminds us of the goal, according to his description of Chopin's playing: "…and everything without the slightest apparent exertion, a pleasing freedom and lightness being a distinguishing characteristic of his style."[21]

---

[21] Ibid., i.

Claude Debussy
First Arabesque

Observations:

Even though the Two Arabesques were written early (1888) in Debussy's career, they show the characteristics of composition that had made him a problem for his theory instructors. He is described in *The International Cyclopedia of Music and Musicians* as having a "feeling for unorthodox chord successions" and engaging in "vehement arguments in opposition to the rules of traditional harmonic procedure."[22]

Objectives:

The musical gesture of curving lines (arabesque) requires a matching flexibility of movement in the body. The two-against-three sections call for complex motor coordination, increased when the right hand has two voices to present as melody and accompaniment. Such subtleties, demanding so much attention, must find their place within the Fundamental Gestures that build the full musical design.

This exercise is related to Exercise 3.4 under Fundamental Gesture:

Variation:

T and S face each other, S holds a scarf in each hand

"Mirror my movements."

T swings arms to the left, starting a horizontal figure eight, and counts "1-2."

T completes figure eight to the right with counts "3-4."

T varies tempo.

"Continue."

---

[22] Oscar Thompson, "Claude Debussy," in *The International Cyclopedia of Music and Musicians*. 7th ed., ed., Nicholas Slonimsky (New York: Dodd, Mead and Co., 1956), 413.

T goes to piano and watches S's left arm, so as to begin playing in time with the circular movement.

T plays through the first five bars, or farther, if desired.

T and S reverse roles.

Reflections:

Did S's arm movements become free and flexible?

Did S explore space?

Did S's eyes follow the scarves?

Did S follow the *ritard* in bar 5 with a larger movement?

In m. 6, Debussy introduces the polyrhythm two-against-three, which becomes a major pattern throughout the piece. The following exercise in a variation of Exercise 3.20 under Counterpoint:

Preparation:

T and S stand facing each other, palms up.

"Clap your hands in groups of 3."

T encourages arm flexibility by moving arms in shape of triangle.

"Clap twice on '2.'"

"Leave out the first clap on '2.'"

"Leave out '3.'"

"Go back to '1-2-3.'"

"Switch."

"And stop."

"Tap your right leg in groups of 3."

"Place each tap higher so that you always reach down for '1.'"

"Continue."

T holds out one palm.

"With your left hand, tap '1' on my hand."

T holds out both palms.

"Tap my other hand between '2' and '3.'"

S moves left arm back and forth between T's hands.

"Take these motions to the keyboard."

"Play notes of a triad with the right hand on '1-2-3.'"

"Play a broken octave in the left hand on '1' and between '2.'"

"And stop."

Reflections:

When clapping, was S's whole body flexible (check the knees)?

Did you change dynamics in your voice and taps for variety?

Remember that this complex pattern must become a Fundamental Gesture, with arms and shoulders shifting slightly with the flow of the music.

Objective:

The middle section of the First Arabesque finds much of its energy and charm in long notes, starting on the second beat. These are not difficult to play in time, but they must convey a lift that carries the music over the third beat.

Preparation:

> T with drum, S ready to step
>
> **"Step gently with my taps and sway from one foot to the other."**
>
> **"Go."**
>
> T taps drum and counts "1-2-3-4."
>
> **"Let your arms join in the sway."**
>
> After this movement has become comfortable, T gives a new command.
>
> **"Lift your knee on 3, then step on 4."**
>
> S lifts knee in a curve and touches the floor again on 4.
>
> **"1-2-lift-4."**
>
> **"Let your arms help you lift."**
>
> Changing the placement of the lift to different beats is an exercise in concentration and flexibility which can be useful in any composition with notes longer than a beat.
>
> **"Lift on 2."**
>
> **"1-lift-3-4-turn."**
>
> **"And stop."**

Reflections:

> Did S's body continue to move through the air over beat 3? "Freezing" on beat 2 will not carry the music over beat 3 and on to beat 4.
>
> Did S's whole body get involved in direction changes, so that they were fluid?

(The movement side to side permits using full body weight in a small space. If you have more room, S can move freely in any direction.)

Apply the same physical feeling of lift and stretch throughout bars 89-95, especially when an eighth is tied over the barline and needs all the help it can get to hold up the melodic line. Half notes in a syncopation do not feel like half notes which begin on the first or third beat. Because they are in a rhythmic spot where the energy is usually a little low, as in the recovery moment after a push, a half note on beat 2 must put out extra energy to overcome the natural deficit AND send the melody forward.

Béla Bartók
Dance in Bulgarian Rhythm
Mikrokosmos **Vol. 6, No. 148**

Observations:

The six volumes of the *Mikrokosmos* provide us with an amazing collection of pieces, ranging from the five-finger compositions in Vol. 1 to the advanced recital works of Vol. 6. They were written late in Bartók's career (1937).

Objectives:

This dance, based on a typical Bulgarian rhythm, derives its energy from a fast pulse, which underlies the accents of the movement. The groups, marked by the accents, vary in specific patterns; in this case, 4 + 2 + 3. The pattern forms a flow of beats of irregular length which pushes forward into larger musical gestures. Expressing these with verve and liveliness depends upon feeling the expansion from the fast pulse to the group pattern to the larger phrase gestures to the cadential sections to the whole rise and fall from beginning to end. See Exercise 3.12 to review unequal beats.

Preparation:

S ready to tap edge of piano or table with all fingers of both hands; T ready to play scale-tones (one hand) ca. MM 250; (adjust to suit S's skills)

"Tap the table at the tempo I play."

T keeps pulse, while changing hands and scales for variety.

"Count in 4's."

"Keep the pulse steady with only one hand."

"Tap '1' with the other hand."

"Keep the pulse steady; count in 3's."

"Tap '1' with the other hand."

"Keep the pulse steady; count in 2's."

"Tap '1' with the other hand."

"Tap whatever group I call."

T calls 2, 3, or 4 on the last pulse of the group, to accustom S to changing.

"And stop."

T lets S rest a moment and sets up next activity.

"With both hands, tap four sets of 4, four sets of 2, four sets of 3."

T plays a light, steady pulse on the piano.

"And go."

As S does last set, T says, "Now three sets."

"Now two."

"Now one set."

"Repeat this last pattern until I say 'Stop.'"

"**And stop.**"

Reflections:

Did you keep the game lively by changing among the 4's, 3's, 2's?

Was your command given on the last pulse, with just enough time for S to change?

Did S maintain a state of attentiveness, without becoming tense?

Remember to increase tempo as S gains confidence.

Did S's arm that tapped "1" move with flexibility?

Did you change which arm tapped pulse and which marked "1"?

Variation:

S and T face each other, hands on knees.

"Tap knees at this tempo."

T says, "Dee-duh-duh-duh" several times and taps knees on "Dee." S joins in.

T moves hands a bit higher on legs and changes to "Dee-duh." S joins in.

T moves hands higher and changes to "Dee-duh-duh." S joins in.

"And stop."

"Join me, as soon as you understand the pattern."

T repeats the moves, doing only one of each: 4-2-3. S joins in.

Reflections:

Did your shoulders stay flexible?

Did you feel gravity pull, as you dropped down to begin the group of 4?

Did S join you quickly, sensing how the pattern progressed?

Did the fast pulses fade into the background, so that you felt primarily three groups of different lengths?

Variation:

S and T face each other, each with a drum

"You tap 4 counts; I tap 2; you tap 3; then I start with 4 again."

"Keep the sequence going."

"Now tap only the '1' of each group."

T and S continue, stepping on "1" and moving about each other, as their bodies pick up the impulse.

"I will play the full pattern; you answer."

T taps 1's of 4, 2, 3, moving the drum to a different place for each tap. S imitates.

Reflections:

Did you change levels, so that the whole body was involved?

Did you keep the drum moving?

Vary the activity by dropping out and letting S do all the tapping and moving.

Did you change dynamics to keep the exercise interesting to the ear?

Did you speak your commands rhythmically?

The aural and kinesthetic memory of the irregular pulse groupings now moves to the piano:

S sits at the piano, T stands nearby with drum.

"With the R.H. play three ascending notes an octave apart."

"Repeat the pattern until I make a change."

"Now play the same pattern ascending with the L.H."

"Both hands at once."

"Let your arms move freely. Accuracy is not important."

"Feel the swing back to the first note."

When the movement is well-established, T adds the drum.

"I will play the fast pause. Play your notes on '1' of every four pulses."

When this movement is reliable rhythmically and performed with a free motion, T changes the groups to three, and to two.

"Now play your first note on '1' of a 4-pulse group, the second a 2-pulse, and the third a 3-pulse group."

"Add scale steps in each group to match the fast pulses."

By this time the arm gesture is strong and S is ready for the scale passages in the composition itself. It is important to keep the long gesture of 4 + 2 + 3 so that, when Bartók has passages with quarter-quarter-dotted quarter, as in the Meno Vivo section, the rhythm not become 2 + 2 + 2 + 3. The second quarter of the 4-pulse group must be an anacrusis from the 4-pulse to the 2-pulse group and not a unit by itself. Strengthening the sensation of 4 + 2 + 3 in the previous helps sustain this rhythmic flow in the composition.

Alberto Ginastera
Suite de danzas criollas, Op. 15, III

Observations:

Ginastera combined the rhythms and melodies of South American popular music with the classical forms of Western European music. Irregular meter, irregular beat, metric transformation, and polyrythms abound, as well as modal melodies, extended tertian sonorities, quartal harmonies, and atonal writing. His compositions present problems for many pianists who are not familiar with the dances and gestures that serve as a basis.

This piece is in 'song form:' A A1 B A2. The melodic writing, with its repetitious, stepwise descent, indicates a piece that could be sung, while its mournful character, highlighted by the use of the aeolian mode, presents a song with indigenous roots. The tempo and dynamic indications need particular attention so that the character of the piece is clear to the listener.

Objectives:

We have chosen four aspects of this piece to discuss: (1) Fundamental Gesture, m. 1, (2) irregular meter, 11/8, (3) polyrhythm and (4) canon.

(1) When one begins with a piece that is so obviously based on song, it is first advisable to sing the melody:

Preparation:

T seated at the piano and S standing, able to see the score, ready to sing.

"Let's sing the melody of mm. 1-4 together on 'la.'"

Many students are reluctant to sing; however, when someone sings with them, the burden is lightened. Eventually, have them sing alone.

While they are singing, say:

"Make a sustained arm movement that fits the melody."

"Sing a little louder now...softer...quicker...slower."

T is preparing S for the tempo rubato and dynamic variations in the piece.

The student can now be asked to play the melody at the piano and maintain the sense of the sustained arm movement used while singing (Fundamental Gesture). Ask the student to try to make the playing match the singing.

"Which is the loudest note (the climax of the passage)?"

Have the students make this apparent in their performance. Make every attempt to accept the response; it is important for students to feel as though they are in control of the expression. If students' choices seem poor, they may often change later on. Their creativity is stimulated when they are offered the opportunity to make their own decisions.

(2) The meter in 11/8 causes problems for pianists because they tend to alter the beats so that they are regular. Ginastera's division into 2 + 2 + 2 + 3 + 2 is often altered to become, 2 + 2 + 2 + 3 + 3.

In order to practice unequal beats, we can make a modification to Exercise 3.12:

Preparation:

T and S facing each other with drums.

"Follow me, 2 beats later."

T strikes the drum twice, so that S realizes the tempo. T moves the drum in a Fundamental Gesture that envelops the 2 beats.

"Three of them."

T plays a group of 3 beats, playing each beat at the same tempo as before.

T and S exchange 3-beat and 2-beat groups at T's discretion.

"And stop."

"Either of us can decide to switch from 2 to 3."

"Say 'Two things' or 'Three of them' as you play."

T begins, and S and T exchange irregular beats.

"When I say 'Out,' tap the first of the group (group of 2 or 3)."

"When I say 'In,' tap all the beats."

Continue this study with walking steps, so that the whole body can sense the irregular beats within the Fundamental Gesture. Here is a possible 'dance':

Preparation:

T demonstrates "grapevine step": With feet parallel, move laterally, so that one foot steps behind the other and alternately in front of the other.

"L. step behind, R. step L. cross in front, R. step." (Repeat.)

Shift weight to L. R. step, L. cross in front. Now R. is ready to step behind and reverse direction.

"Reverse direction."

Moving laterally, cross L behind R, step R to right; cross L in front of R, step R to right (4 beats).

Repeat (4 more beats).

Shift weight to L (1 beat) and repeat pattern to the left, leading with cross R behind L.

The student can now return to singing the melody (mm. 1-4), while tapping all the inner beats, and then, just the first beats of the group. The larger grouping of 2 and 3 (Subordinate Gesture) should be clear, even though the student is tapping the inner beats.

(3) The polyrhythm occurs in the first part of most of the measures: the left hand accentuates counts 1 and 4 of 6/8 and the right hand promotes a duple division. Before addressing the polyrhythm in this piece, we will return to Exercise 3.23, which provides a general exercise for two-against-three in counterpoint:

Preparation:

T and S facing each other, both with drums.

"Follow me, one bar later."

T counts 6 beats out loud, while tapping on 1 and 4.

T strikes two different places on the drum, maintaining a continuous flow.

T stops, while S imitates ("interrupted canon").

T continues pattern several times.

Bass Melody

"And stop."

"Follow me, one bar later."

T counts 6 beats aloud, while tapping on 1, 3, and 5.

T strikes three different places on the drum, maintaining a slow tempo.

T stops; S imitates, while counting out loud ("interrupted canon").

T continues pattern several times.

"Maintain this pattern, while I change."

Teacher returns to first pattern.

"When I say 'Change,' change to my pattern."

T calls "Change" at regular and then irregular intervals.

"And stop."

"Tap and count out loud on 1, 3, and 5."

"Keep tapping the drum on 1, 3, and 5."

"Count on 1 and 4."

"When I say 'Switch,' reverse roles."

"You decide when to switch."

"And stop."

Have the student sing the melody in m. 1 and play the three concurrent bass notes in m. 1, D-E-F-sharp. Next, have the student play the RH melody and sing the bass. The student should notice that the bass has a melody of its own that needs to be brought out.

Finally, play both hands in m. 1. The Fundamental Gesture in this piece involves both upper arms, directing the lower hierarchical movements in contrary motion toward the center of the keyboard. Both arms shape the top arc of a circle as they proceed. This particular motion in this piece conjures up emotions, such as comforting, calming and soothing. The teacher should call on the student to find a personal description of the emotion.

(4) When the smaller motions are securely enveloped in the Fundamental Gesture, the student needs to confront the canon that begins in mm. 5-9. As a review for this problem, we suggest a modification of an exercise, such as Exercise 3.19.

Preparation:

> T and S face each other with drums.

"Follow me, three counts later."

> T plays a subdivided beat pattern (1-5 subdivisions) in 4-beat meter, ("interrupted canon"). S responds.

"Follow me, two counts later."

> Now T changes to "true canon" (if S is ready), so that T continues to perform, while S responds to the previous pattern.

"Follow me, one beat later."

"And stop."

> This exercise prepares the student to develop the concentration necessary to be able to switch listening/playing from one line of the canon to the other. It is difficult to make the melody sing in the left hand, because the thumb is required to play every melody note. Sing the line and try to match the desired expression with the left hand.

> Finally, the student should try to grasp a deeper Fundamental Gesture that helps solidify the background structure, A A1 B A2. For instance, in the A section, begin in a standing position, hear the melody internally and shift the weight from foot to foot for each measure of 11/8. While shifting the weight, introduce a slight spiral throughout the body. For the A1 and B sections, take a step and face a new direction, while repeating movements similar to the A section. Return to the original position for the final A2 section.

AFTERWORD

It is important for students to find their own unique Gestures to serve as choreography for the music. The Gestures should include awareness of all the energy sources: rhythmic flow, including accent and beat location (anacrusis, crusis, metacrusis); pitch location, including height, intervals, scale degree, and accidentals; patterns of repetitions, variations, and contrast; articulation; and the relationships of the parts (Supraficial) to the whole (Fundamental Gesture). This kind of exploration will reveal a personal expression and technique for the piece that the student can project in performance. This ownership of expression empowers the student to convey the emotion to an audience with confidence and conviction.

A music lesson is a three-party conversation: student, teacher, and music. The goal for every hour we are together is to achieve a level of mutual understanding so that all three are, for the moment, breathing together. We, the teachers, have conversed with music. We have listened to its messages of proportion and energy. We have asked questions about its sense of direction and moments of crisis. We have reveled in its joys and let it carry us into darkness. We know the power of music.

Our students come to us because they, too, have become fascinated with sounds. How often have we had a mother, inquiring about lessons for her child, say, "He can't keep his hands off the piano," "She sings all the time." At this moment, the child is really conversing with music, responding to the flow of music. When we have the privilege of assisting this fascination by developing mastery over the materials of music, we must not lose the fascination. Delight in sound—pitch, duration, dynamics, repetition and contrast—is a precious commodity and easily spoiled by unmusical drill. We must achieve at every lesson moments of truly expressive performance. A moment may be only two bars, but they are two bars that have been expressed musically and have been listened to with appreciation and joy.

The goal of communicative music guided Dalcroze's work, as he developed his approach. He strove to heighten musical expression, so that performer and listener heard the message in the flow of the music throughout the whole performance. His experiments, expanded over fifty years, convinced him that the way to accomplish this was to bring the whole body into play, the mind into attentiveness, and the spirit into a state of sensitivity and flexibility.

In this book, we have tried, through discussion and description, to present ways of keeping the conversation going between teacher, student and music. Those of us who use this approach know that it brings us to musical performance in a direct and efficient way. We know that moments spent away from the instrument, exploring the sensation of the music, brings immediate results in performance.

The stories from our own students describe activities that grew out of situations common to all teaching, yet unique in detail to that student and that piece of music and that teacher and that studio space. Our endeavor has been to give you so many examples that you can tease out the principles which underlie the activities themselves. It is essential that the games we have described not be taken as formulas: They are starting points for your own experiments. Trying them out will give you the experience of listening to your body and feeling how the energy moves. You will quickly find ways to vary them, keeping the basic principles of continuity, variation, focus and musicality. The principles should help you develop the freedom to improvise activities that will highlight the musical problem of the moment. Even using the same activity—swishing of scarves, for instance—will have different results with different students and different music. As long as the movement clarifies the musical moment, it is right! Some activities will not be effective. (I have sometimes designed a new pattern while sitting at a desk, only to discover, when I stood up and tried the steps, that it just didn't work. The body weight couldn't move as I had thought, or the movement was too complicated for the tempo I envisioned.) Often, a small tweak will cause the activity to reveal the musical effect you are searching for.

Listen to your students. They will give you leads for improvement, sometimes by suggesting them, sometimes by a failure which alerts you to a different way of approaching the same idea, sometimes by performing so well, so easily, that you know you need to develop more challenge. Being responsive to the students' situation—to their anxiety, their enthusiasm and their success—will expand your own creativity. If you keep in mind the three aspects of human experience—body, mind, and spirit—you will foster in your students a balanced approach to musical understanding.

When these three elements of experience are equally strong, equally aware and responsive, pleasure in performance will flower. Students play with increased confidence when they understand their music mentally, physically, and emotionally. This level of confidence also encourages a social confidence, an aspect which Dalcroze noticed as his program developed. Feeling the body under control and feeling it move smoothly, with expressive gestures, is a truly empowering state of being. Lessons develop a certain spontaneity and immediacy that lifts the necessary learning of note names, keys, meter signatures and rhythm patterns, as well as scale degrees and harmonic relationships, into musical games. This constant invoking of physical feeling lifts routine study into a state of musical delight. Such an approach brings students to a level of confidence in their performance, their physical power, their mental capacity, and their feelings, which they are willing to express for their own pleasure and that of others, as well.

Every time you invent ways to move away from the instrument and use the whole body in expressing the beat and the phrase and the Fundamental Gesture, you will feel a growing appreciation for the variety of ways you can teach. Even in a small space, when both teacher and student stand and bounce knees for the beat, when you direct the student to sing the melody to your drum accompaniment, when you both stretch to one side and then the other to express the legato quality of the phrase, you both feel physical relief and refreshment. Teacher and student together benefit from these momentary changes.

Be bold! Leap into the unpredictable and explore the possibilities. When done in a spirit of exploration—"Let's see what will happen if we try it this way!"—your creative physical activities will expand the number of avenues of learning and will stimulate excitement, pleasure, and learning on a profound, unforgettable level.